亚运文化之旅

杭州亚运会参赛国家和地区文化知识双语绘本

杭州城市国际化研究院文创工作室　编绘

前 言

亚洲幅员辽阔、历史悠久，国家和地区众多，是人类文明的重要起源地，创造了璀璨的历史文化，留下了丰富的世界遗产。亚洲国家和地区风土人情独特多元，生活方式、思想观念、文化艺术、饮食风味等各有特色。

本书针对目前有关亚运文化、亚洲文化大众读物稀少的现象，借杭州亚运会契机，着力展现亚洲文明多姿多彩的文化内涵。本书以杭州亚运会45个参赛国家和地区为描述对象，多维度收集、筛选、梳理亚运会参赛国家和地区的自然地理、人文风貌，尤其是标志性建筑、生活习俗、体育项目等方面的知识，以图画展示为核心，配以双语解读，介绍相关国家和地区的主要特色，增进大众对于亚洲地区历史文化的了解，促进不同文明相互尊重、互学互鉴、共同发展。

本书按地理区域划分，以东亚、东南亚、南亚、中亚和西亚五大区域对杭州亚运会45个参赛国家和地区进行内容编排。在整体布局上，每个国家和地区的内容均由两部分构成：一是国家和地区简明扼要的文字介绍；二是以图文形式展现各个国家和地区的自然地理、标志性建筑、传统运动、饮食文化等内容。

本书图文并茂、雅俗共赏，以图像化的方式鲜活地呈现亚洲国家和地区的悠久文化和风土人情，并配以简明的中英双语解读，使读者快速了解亚运会参赛国家和地区的文化特色。本书既可作为亚运会的配套科普读物，也可作为中小学生的课外读物。

Preface

Asia, with its vast territory, long history, and multitudinous countries, stands as an important cradle of civilization. Asia has created splendid histories and cultures, presenting rich and remarkable cultural heritages. With unique lifestyles, ideas, art and food in each country and region, this marvelous continent becomes a place where diverse customs and pluralistic cultures coexist and thrive.

As the Hangzhou Asian Games approaches, we hope to exhibit the extraordinary cultures of Asia and enhance public understanding of the histories and cultures of Asian countries and regions. Targeting 45 participating countries and regions in the Hangzhou Asian Games, we have collected, selected and sorted out relevant knowledge concerning their natural geography and cultural styles, especially iconic architectures, customs, sports, etc. Combining pictures with bilingual texts, this book introduces the main cultural features of relevant countries and regions, can promote mutual respect, mutual learning and common development among different civilizations.

The format of this book is arranged according to geographical areas, dividing 45 participating countries and regions into five categories: East Asia, Southeast Asia, South Asia, Central Asia and West Asia. In terms of overall layout, the content of each country or region consists of two parts: the first part is a concise bilingual introduction of the place and the second part is an illustration reflecting its natural geography, architecture, sports and cuisine.

Rich in pictures and texts, this book can be enjoyed by both experts and general readers. Together with brief interpretations, the long-standing cultures and folk customs of Asian countries and regions are vividly presented in a graphic and visual manner, inviting readers to comprehend the cultural characteristics of 45 participating countries and regions in a leisure way. This picture book can be utilized both as a popular science book for the Asian Games and as extracurricular reading material for primary and secondary school students.

目 录 Contents

东 亚 East Asia

朝　　鲜　Democratic People's Republic of Korea / 3
韩　　国　Republic of Korea / 7
蒙　　古　Mongolia / 11
日　　本　Japan / 15
中　　国　China / 19
中国澳门　Macao, China / 25
中国台北　Chinese Taipei / 29
中国香港　Hong Kong, China / 33

东南亚 Southeast Asia

东 帝 汶　Timor-Leste / 39
菲 律 宾　Philippines / 43
柬 埔 寨　Cambodia / 47
老　　挝　Laos / 51
马 来 西 亚　Malaysia / 55
缅　　甸　Myanmar / 59
泰　　国　Thailand / 63
文　　莱　Brunei / 67
新 加 坡　Singapore / 71
印度尼西亚　Indonesia / 75
越　　南　Viet Nam / 79

南亚 South Asia

巴基斯坦　Pakistan　85
不　　丹　Bhutan　89
马尔代夫　Maldives　93
孟加拉国　Bangladesh　97
尼 泊 尔　Nepal　101
斯里兰卡　Sri Lanka　105
印　　度　India　109

中亚 Central Asia

哈萨克斯坦　Kazakhstan　115
吉尔吉斯斯坦　Kyrgyzstan　119
塔吉克斯坦　Tajikistan　123
土库曼斯坦　Turkmenistan　127
乌兹别克斯坦　Uzbekistan　131

西亚 West Asia

阿　富　汗　Afghanistan / 137
阿拉伯联合酋长国　The United Arab Emirates / 141
阿　　　曼　Oman / 145
巴 勒 斯 坦　Palestine / 149
巴　　　林　Bahrain / 153
卡　塔　尔　Qatar / 157
科　威　特　Kuwait / 161
黎　巴　嫩　Lebanon / 165
沙特阿拉伯　Saudi Arabia / 169
叙　利　亚　Syria / 173
也　　　门　Yemen / 177
伊　拉　克　Iraq / 181
伊　　　朗　Iran / 185
约　　　旦　Jordan / 189

后记 Afterword

致谢 Acknowledgement

东 亚 East Asia

朝 鲜
Democratic People's Republic of Korea

全称朝鲜民主主义人民共和国。朝鲜位于朝鲜半岛北半部，雄伟的劳动党建党纪念塔和中朝友谊塔是首都平壤的城市地标。金日成广场临大同江而建。大型艺术表演《阿里郎》演绎着朝鲜的传统文化，传唱至今。

朝鲜流行的运动项目有足球、马拉松、篮球等。

Full name: Democratic People's Republic of Korea. Democratic People's Republic of Korea is in north Korean Peninsula. The Monument to Party Founding and Sino-Korean Friendship Tower are landmarks of the capital city Pyongyang. The Kim Il-sung Square sits in front of the Taedong River. The musical play *Arirang* demonstrates Korean tradition and is still popular today.

Football, marathon, basketball, etc. are popular in Democratic People's Republic of Korea.

中朝友谊塔

朝鲜人民为铭记中国人民志愿军烈士们的丰功伟绩，于志愿军入朝参战 9 周年之际建成，塔下的浮雕表现了中朝人民并肩作战的友谊。

Sino-Korean Friendship Tower

Completed on the ninth anniversary of the Chinese People's Volunteer Army's arrival in Democratic People's Republic of Korea, the Sino-Korean Friendship Tower is built in memory of the heroic sacrifices of the Army. The sculptures on the tower depict the scene that Democratic People's Republic of Korea and the People's Republic of China were fighting together, commemorating the friendship formed in the battlefield.

金日成广场

朝鲜首都平壤的中央广场，是举行重要政治文化活动的场所。

Kim Il-sung Square

Kim Il-sung Square, a large city square in the central district of Pyongyang, is a gathering place for rallies, dances, and parades.

平壤建党纪念塔

位于首都平壤的中轴线上，朝鲜劳动党成立 50 周年（1995）之际建成。由象征工人、农民和知识分子之手紧攥的锤子、镰刀和毛笔的塔身组成。

Monument to Party Founding

Located on the axis across the center of Pyongyang, the monument was officially completed in 1995. It consists of a hammer, a sickle, and a calligraphy brush which are tightly held in three hands, symbolizing workers, farmers and intellectuals respectively.

朝鲜跳板游戏

朝鲜妇女喜爱的一种传统娱乐活动，在长条木板正中垫木架一块，两端各站一人，一方首先跳起，靠下落的冲击力将对方弹向空中，一起一落之际，做出各种动作。

Neolttwigi

Neolttwigi is a traditional outdoor game that is popular among Korean girls and women. Neolttwigi is similar to seesaw, except that participants stand on each end of the Neol (board) and jump, propelling the person opposite into the air with acrobatic tricks.

东 亚 East Asia

金达莱

朝鲜国花，象征着朝鲜人民坚韧不拔、不畏艰险的民族精神。

Azaleas

Azaleas is Democratic People's Republic of Korea's national flower. Azaleas symbolizes local people's strong will and pure spirit.

苍鹰

朝鲜国鸟，其刚毅勇敢的精神为朝鲜人民所喜爱。

Northern Goshawk

The northern goshawk, Democratic People's Republic of Korea's national bird, is honored by the locals because of its imposing figure and fighting spirit.

大同江啤酒

朝鲜最受欢迎的啤酒品牌，于2002年开业，以大同江为水源，故名。

Taedonggang Beer

Taedonggang is the top beer brand in Democratic People's Republic of Korea. Opened in 2002, the Taedonggang Beer Factory was named after the Taedong River, and it uses the water to produce the beer.

冷面

以荞麦面、牛肉、胡萝卜等材料制作而成，是朝鲜族传统食品。

Cold Noodles

Cold noodles is a traditional Korean noodle dish with long and thin noodles made from the buckwheat flour, usually served with beef and carrots.

泡菜

朝鲜族特色小吃，以白菜、萝卜等蔬菜为主原料，加上种类繁多的调味料，经乳酸发酵而成。

Kimchi

Kimchi is one of the locals' favorite traditional side dishes made with cabbage, radish and a wide variety of seasonings, through lactic acid fermentation.

韩 国
Republic of Korea

全称大韩民国。韩国位于朝鲜半岛南半部，三面环海。韩国国旗也称"太极旗"。首尔的德寿宫融合了东西方的建筑元素，京畿道水原华城诉说着古老的故事。传统与现代文化碰撞，韩国讲述着自己的亚洲故事，韩国美食吸引着来自世界各地的食客。

韩国举办过汉城（今首尔）亚运会（1986）、汉城（今首尔）奥运会（1988）、釜山亚运会（2002）、仁川亚运会（2014）和平昌冬奥会（2018）。跆拳道是韩国流行的一项体育运动。

Full name: Republic of Korea. Lying in the southern part of the Korean Peninsula, Republic of Korea is bounded by sea on three sides. The philosophy of Yin and Yang is reflected in the pattern of Republic of Korea's national flag. Deoksugung Palace in Seoul is an excellent exhibition of the combination of both eastern and western architectural styles. Ancient forts in Gyeonggi Province tell the ancient stories. Republic of Korea narrates its own Asian story by merging tradition with modern culture. Modern cuisine here appeals to gourmets all around the world.

Republic of Korea held the Seoul Asian Games (1986), Seoul Summer Olympic Games (1988), Busan Asian Games (2002), Incheon Asian Games (2014) and Pyeongchang Winter Olympic Games (2018). Taekwondo is a popular sport in Republic of Korea.

N 首尔塔

位于首尔龙山区南山，是韩国著名的观光景点。"N"既是南山（Namsan）的第一个字母，又有"全新"（New）的含义。夜幕降临，塔上有六盏探照灯在天空中拼出鲜花盛开的图案——首尔之花。

N Seoul Tower

The N Seoul Tower, an attraction of Republic of Korea, is located in Namsan Mountain in central Seoul. The letter N represents "new" and "Namsan". In the evening, six LED searchlights on the tower shine to the sky, delineating an image of a flower, which is called "the flower of Seoul".

德寿宫

位于首尔繁华的街道上，以富有特色的石墙路而闻名。在首尔的宫殿中，德寿宫是唯一一座中西结合的宫殿建筑。

Deoksugung Palace

Located on a populous street, Deoksugung Palace is known for its stone wall road. The Palace is the only existent palace in Seoul which contains both eastern and western architecture.

济州岛石像

济州岛多产黑灰色火山石，用它雕刻成的守护神被当地人亲切地叫作"石头爷爷"。

Dol Hareubangs

Dol hareubangs are large statues carved from volcanic rocks on the Jeju Island. The name derives from the Korean word for "stone", plus the Jeju dialect word hareubang, meaning "grandfather".

水原华城

李朝（1392—1910）后期建于京畿道水原市内的邑城，堪称东方城郭的典范，世界文化遗产。

Hwaseong Fortress

The Hwaseong Fortress was a city built in the late Li Dynasty (1392-1910) in Suwon City of Gyeonggi Province. The fortress is regarded as a model of oriental cities and it is now one of the World Cultural Heritage Sites.

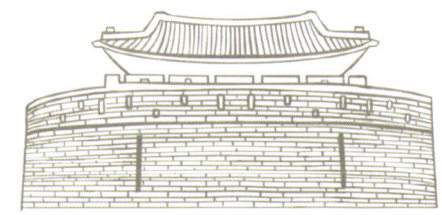

东 亚 East Asia

韩国民族舞蹈

在韩国传统农业文化的基础上形成，其特点是古典与现代并存。

Korean Traditional Dance
The Korean traditional dance originated in the ancient agricultural civilization. It is characterized by the coexistence of the classical and modern.

太极虎

虎在韩国人的心目中是神兽。1986年汉城（今首尔）亚运会的吉祥物是太极虎多里。

Hodori
The image of tiger is holy to the Korean. Hodori was the official mascot of the 1986 Asian Games in Seoul, Republic of Korea.

木槿花

一种生命力很强的花，象征着韩国人民坚韧不拔的民族性格。

Mugunghwa
Mugunghwa has a nickname as "the eternal flower" because of its long bloom and strong life. As the national flower, it symbolizes the Republic of Korea's nationality of persistence and diligence.

韩服

韩国传统服饰，融合了中国汉服和韩国本土服饰的特征。

Hanbok
The traditional Korean clothes hanbok integrates the characteristics of Chinese Hanfu and Korean dresses.

蒙 古
Mongolia

全称蒙古国。蒙古是位于亚洲中部的内陆国。蓝色的库苏古尔湖旁,牛羊像珍珠般散落在草原上。现代与传统在首都乌兰巴托交融,蒙古包是传统的住宅形式,延续至今。原野上的敖包旁,那达慕大会传承着蒙古民族独具特色的集体娱乐活动。

蒙古流行的体育项目有摔跤、赛马、射箭等。

Full name: Mongolia. Mongolia is a landlocked country in central Asia. Cattle and sheep are like pearls all over the pasture by the blue Lake Huvsgol. Modernity intertwines with tradition in the young city Ulan Bator, and the yurt keeps the traditional residential form of the Mongolians. Around ovoos, Naadam passes on the unique sports of the nation.

Wrestling, horse racing and archery, etc. are popular sports of the country.

敖包

　　蒙古语，意为"堆子"，原指在辽阔的草原上人们用石头、土、草等堆成的道路和边界的标志，后来逐步演变成祭祀山神、路神和祈祷丰收、家人幸福平安的象征。

Ovoo

Ovoos are stones, soil, grass, etc. heaps primarily used as signposts and landmarks and later as altars or shrines in Mongolian folk religious practice. In the ovoo ceremony, the Mongols pray to the mountain deity and the road deity for the harvest and family happiness.

蒙古包

　　蒙古族牧民居住的一种房子，便于建造和搬迁，适于牧业生产和游牧生活。蒙古包呈圆顶，以厚毡覆盖，冬暖夏凉。

Mongolian Yurt

The Mongolian yurt or ger is a portable, round tent covered with skins or felt, and is used as a nomadic dwelling for nomadic life. Yurts are warm in winter and cool in summer.

东 亚 East Asia

摔跤

蒙古传统的体育运动之一。蒙古人把摔跤称作"搏克"（蒙古语，意为结实、团结和持久）。

Mongolian Wrestling
Mongolian wrestling is the folk wrestling style of the Mongols, known as Bökh, which means strength, union and durability.

赛马

蒙古族被誉为马背上的民族，赛马是男女老少喜爱的活动，赛马又分为跑马、走马和颠马。

Horse Racing
The Mongols are known as the people on horseback. Horse racing, consists of horse running, horse trotting and horse jolting, is a popular sport in which almost everyone participates.

蒙古烤肉

蒙古特色食物，将牛羊肉放在架子上，用火烧烤。

Mongolian Barbecue
Mongolian barbecue is a specialty of Mongolia. Beef and lamb are placed on a shelf and grilled over fire.

日本
Japan

全称日本国。日本是位于太平洋西岸上的岛国，其文化融合了现代与传统，东亚特色浓厚。富士山巍然屹立，在姬路城可以一探日式宫殿韵味。着和服、饮清酒、品寿司，日本民众依然坚守民族习俗。

日本举办过东京亚运会（1958）、东京奥运会（1964、2020）、札幌冬奥会（1972）、广岛亚运会（1994）、长野冬奥会（1998），名古屋将举办2026年亚运会。日本的传统体育项目有相扑、剑道等。

Full name: Japan. Japan, an island country in the Pacific Ocean in East Asia, brings a distinguished East Asian culture with both modernity and tradition. On Honshu Island, Mount Fuji rises proudly; in Himeji Castle, one could have a glimpse of typical Japanese palace. Kimono, sake, and sushi are the essence of Japanese ethnic customs.

Japan hosted Tokyo Asian Games (1958), Tokyo Summer Olympic Games (1964, 2020), Sapporo Winter Olympic Games (1972), Hiroshima Asian Games (1994), Nagano Winter Olympic Games (1998). The 20th Asian Games will be held in Nagoya in 2026. Traditional sports in Japan include sumo and kendo, etc.

富士山

一座横跨静冈县和山梨县的活火山，是日本的最高峰，也是日本的重要象征之一。

Mount Fuji

Mount Fuji is an active volcano straddling the boundary of Shizuoka and Yamanashi Prefectures. It is the highest mountain in Japan and is a distinctive symbol of Japan.

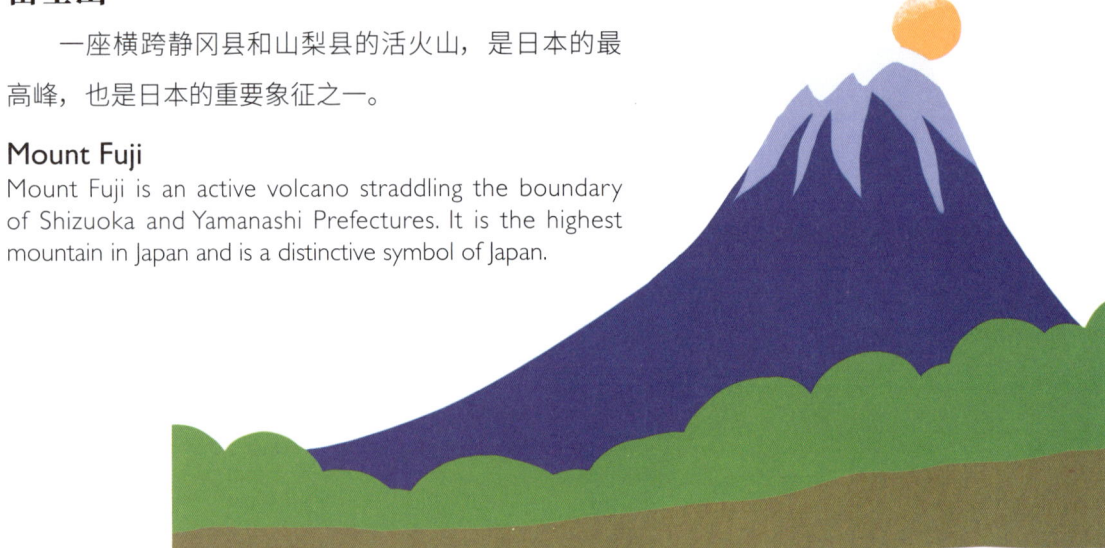

姬路城

一座位于姬路市的城堡，有白色的外墙，也被称为白鹭城。由于保存完好，它被称为"日本第一名城"。

Himeji Castle

Himeji Castle is a Japanese castle located in Himeji City. Its white plastered earthen walls have earned it the name White Heron Castle. It is also called "the first premier castle in Japan" for its fine preservation.

和服

日本的传统民族服饰，为平面裁剪制成的宽松袍服。

Kimono

The kimono is a traditional Japanese garment which is a loose robe made of flat cutting.

东 亚 East Asia

樱花

日本民族的象征。樱花的花期很短，边开边落，它象征着高雅、质朴的品格。

Sakura

Sakura, known as Japanese cherry, is considered as the symbol of Japanese nation. The flowering period of cherry blossoms is very short. Cherry blossom symbolizes elegant and simple character.

清酒

借鉴中国黄酒的酿造法而发展起来的日本国酒，酒色清亮透明。日本人常说，清酒是神的恩赐。

Sake

Clear and transparent, the sake developed by borrowing the brewing method of rice wine in China is the national wine of Japan. The Japanese often say that sake is a gift from the gods.

寿司

日本传统美食，以用醋调味过的冷饭为主要材料，加上鱼虾、蔬菜或鸡蛋等做配料，将这些食材平铺在紫菜片上卷成条，切成小段食用。

Sushi

Sushi, a traditional Japanese delicacy, features chilled rice seasoned with vinegar, complemented by an array of toppings such as fish, shrimps, vegetables, or eggs. These ingredients are then wrapped in seaweed slices, rolled into strips, and cut into small pieces.

中 国
China

全称中华人民共和国。中国历史文化悠久，中华文明璀璨夺目。万里长城是世界文化遗产，也是人类文明的财富；天安门是新中国的象征；憨态可掬的大熊猫是中国特有的珍贵动物。杭州奥体中心体育场（大莲花）是第19届亚运会、第4届亚残运会的主会场；三潭印月是杭州"西湖第一胜境"；大运河拱宸桥象征着"连通"与"友谊"，代表着对五湖四海宾朋的欢迎和敬意。

中国举办过北京亚运会（1990）、北京奥运会（2008）、广州亚运会（2010）和北京冬奥会（2022）等体育赛事。中国传统体育项目有武术、射箭、摔跤、龙舟、舞狮等。

Full name: the People's Republic of China. With its long history, Chinese culture is thriving and splendid. The Great Wall is the World Cultural Heritage Site and the wealth of human civilization. Tian'anmen is the symbol of modern China and the giant panda is the Chinese national treasure. Hangzhou Olympic Sports Center Stadium (the Big Lotus) is the main stadium for the 19th Asian Games and the 4th Asian Para Games. In Hangzhou, Three Pools Mirroring the Moon is honored as "the first scenic spot of the West Lake". Standing for "connectivity" and "friendship", the Gongchen Bridge across the Grand Canal welcomes guests and friends around the world.

China held Beijing Asian Games (1990), Beijing Summer Olympic Games (2008), Guangzhou Asian Games (2010) and Beijing Winter Olympic Games (2022). Traditional Chinese sports include wushu, archery, wrestling, dragon boat, lion dance, etc.

天安门

坐落在中华人民共和国首都北京市的中心、故宫的南端。天安门曾经是明清两代皇城的正门，由城台和城楼两部分组成。天安门上悬挂着国徽和毛泽东主席像，是新中国的象征，也是中华人民共和国举行重大国事的场所。

Tian'anmen

Tian'anmen stands in the center of China's capital city, Beijing, to the south of the Palace Museum. It was the front entrance to the Forbidden City which was the imperial palace of the Ming and Qing Dynasties. It consists of two parts: the castle platform and the castle tower. With the national emblem and the portrait of Chairman Mao hanging on it, Tian'anmen symbolizes modern China and is the venue for major state events of China.

长城

又称"万里长城"，是中国古代伟大的军事性防御工程。一道以城墙为主体的绵延不断的墙垣，与大量的城、障、亭、标相结合，构成防御体系，以阻隔游牧部落的侵犯。始建于战国时期，秦统一中国后，连接和修缮长城，始有"万里长城"之称。长城是世界历史上伟大的工程之一，被列入《世界遗产名录》。

The Great Wall

The Great Wall, an ancient Chinese military defense project, comprised a continuous wall with city walls as its main body. It integrated castles, barricades, pavilions, and signs, forming a formidable defense system against nomadic tribal aggression. Initially constructed during the Warring States Period, the walls were later interconnected under the unification of China by the Qin Dynasty. As one of history's monumental projects, the Great Wall holds a prestigious place on the *Word Heritage List*.

东 亚 East Asia

大熊猫

中国特有的珍贵动物，主要栖息在四川、陕西和甘肃省内的茂密竹林里，体色黑白相间，被誉为"活化石"和"中国国宝"，属国家一级保护动物。

Giant Panda

The giant panda is a rare species of China. It mainly inhabits dense bamboo forests in Sichuan, Shaanxi and Gansu Provinces. Its body color is black and white. Known as the "living fossil" and "Chinese national treasure", the giant panda is the first class protected animal in China.

竹

中国盛产竹子，素有"竹子王国"之美誉。竹挺拔、修长，四季青翠，备受中国人喜爱。竹与梅、兰、菊并称"花中四君子"，与梅、松并称"岁寒三友"。

Bamboo

China is rich in bamboo and is known as the "Kingdom of Bamboo". Loved by Chinese people, bamboo is tall, slender and verdant in all seasons. Bamboo, plum, orchid and chrysanthemum are called the "four gentlemen of flowers". Meanwhile, bamboo, plum and pine are respected as the "three friends in chilly weather".

杭州奥体中心体育场

俗称"大莲花"，选取莲花为造型原型，由28片大花瓣和27片小花瓣组成，荣获中国建筑行业工程质量最高奖项鲁班奖及国家科学技术进步奖一等奖。大莲花作为第19届亚运会主体育场，将承办开、闭幕式和田径比赛项目。

Hangzhou Olympic Sports Center Stadium

The stadium is also commonly called "the Big Lotus" for its lotus-shaped appearance. Consisting of 28 large petals and 27 small petals, it won the Luban Prize, the highest award in the field of architectural quality, and the first prize of the National Science and Technology Progress Award. As the main stadium for the 19th Asian Games, "the Big Lotus" will host the opening and closing ceremonies as well as track and field competitions.

三潭印月

杭州西湖十景之一，被誉为"西湖第一胜境"。三潭印月是西湖中最大的岛屿，具有湖中有岛、岛中有湖、园中有园、曲回多变、步移景新的江南水上庭园特色。岛南湖面上有三座石塔鼎足而立，每当月明之夜，石塔圆洞灯烛投影，水面光影点点，形成月照塔、塔映月的绮丽景象，故得名"三潭印月"。

Three Pools Mirroring the Moon

As one of the ten scenic spots of the West Lake in Hangzhou, Three Pools Mirroring the Moon is known as "the first scenic spot of the West Lake". As the largest island in the West Lake, it combines the characteristics of Jiangnan gardens with island in the lake, lake in the island and garden in the garden. Three stone towers stand on the lake in the south of the island. Whenever the moon is overhead, the stone towers are projected with candles in the round holes, and the water surface is dotted with light and shadow, forming a beautiful scene of the moon shining on the towers and the towers reflecting the moon, hence the name.

拱宸桥

位于杭州市拱墅区，横跨大运河，是杭州现存古桥中最高最长的石拱桥，京杭大运河南端的独特标志与文化符号，也是中国大运河世界文化遗产的遗产点之一。该桥全长 98 米，桥身用条石错缝砌筑，上贯穿长锁石，桥面呈柔和弧形，桥体巍峨高大，气魄雄伟。

Gongchen Bridge

Located in Gongshu District, Hangzhou City, the Gongchen Bridge spans the Grand Canal from east to west. As the tallest and longest ancient stone arch bridge in Hangzhou, it is a unique symbol and cultural icon of the southern end of the Beijing-Hangzhou Grand Canal, also one of the World Cultural Heritage Sites of the Grand Canal of China. With the length of 98 meters, the bridge is bodied with the stone staggered masonry, and is noted for its soft curve and magnificent shape.

东 亚 East Asia

太极拳

一种内外兼修、刚柔相济的中国传统拳术。中华人民共和国成立后，太极拳作为强身健体的表演项目和体育比赛项目出现。中国传统太极拳主要有陈氏、杨氏、武氏、吴氏、孙氏等派别，是一个深受人们喜爱的体育运动项目。2020年，"太极拳"被列为世界级非物质文化遗产。

Taiji

Taiji, a traditional Chinese boxing art, is based on the traditional Taoist philosophies of Taiji and Yin-Yang dialectic philosophy. Taiji appeared as a performance event and sports competition to strengthen the body after the founding of the People's Republic of China. Major Taiji schools include Chen, Yang, Wǔ, Wú, Sun schools. In 2020, this beloved sport was listed as a world-class intangible cultural heritage.

霹雳舞

20世纪70年代开始流行的一种街头舞蹈形式，起源于美国的Hip-Hop文化。杭州2022年第19届亚运会正式确立霹雳舞为比赛项目。

Breaking

As a form of street dancing, breaking was rooted in American Hip-Hop culture and became popular in the 1970s. It is officially nominated as a medal event in the 19th Asian Games Hangzhou 2022.

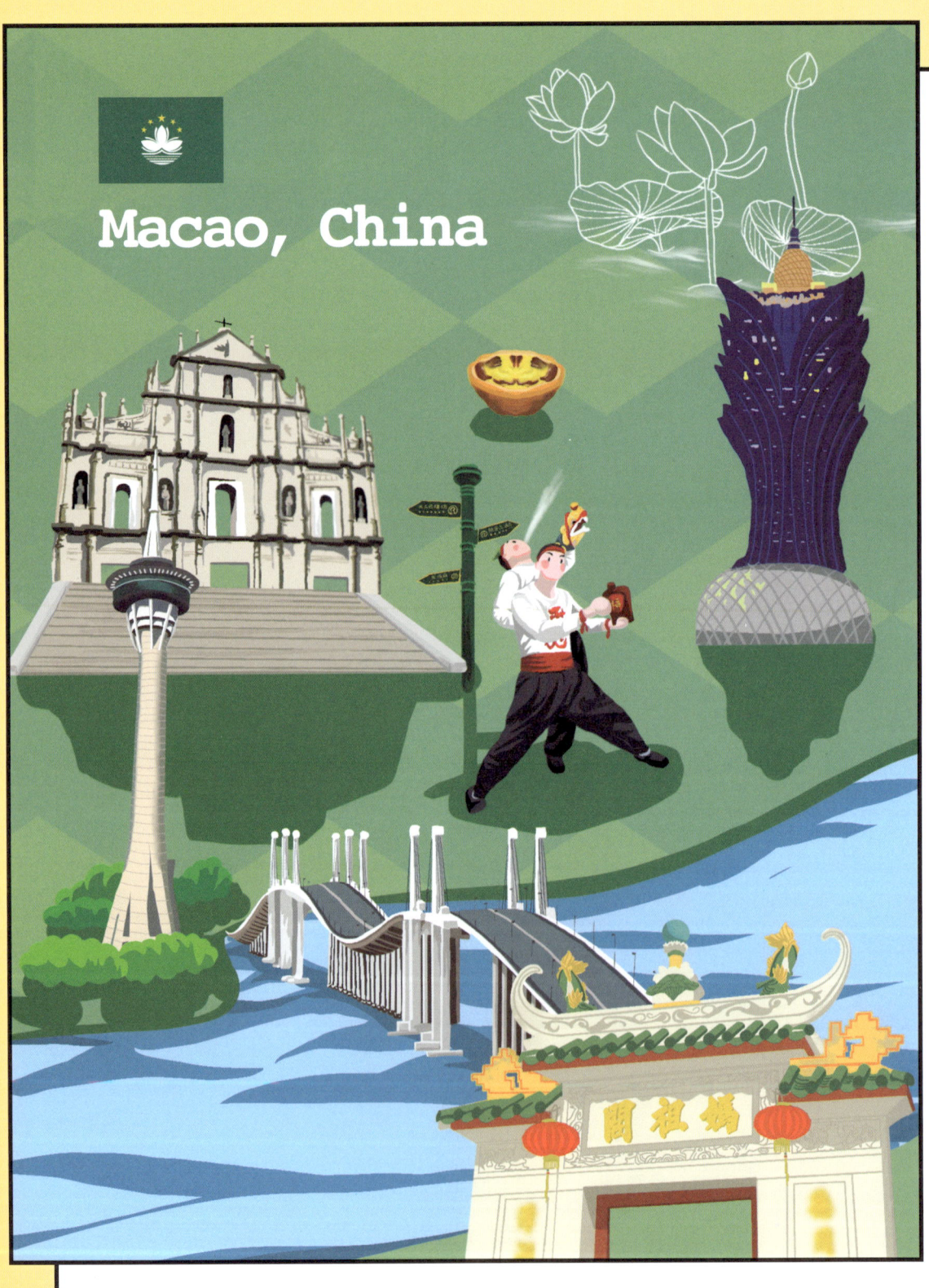

中国澳门
Macao, China

全称中华人民共和国澳门特别行政区。澳门地处中国南部,包括澳门半岛、氹仔岛和路环岛。众多历史遗产展现了澳门独特的文化风情,繁荣经济助力古老"莲岛"焕然一新。著名地标大三巴牌坊亲历澳门时代变迁,新葡京酒店点亮城市夜空,友谊大桥如长虹般横跨海洋。热闹鱼市里,鱼行醉龙节的表演传承澳门特有的民间习俗。宽阔海岸边,妈祖阁象征澳门人数百年来的信仰。

澳门流行的运动项目是传统武术和曲棍球。

Full name: the Macao Special Administrative Region of the People's Republic of China. Located in south China, Macao consists of the Macao Peninsula, Taipa Island and Coloane Island. Numerous historical heritages display the distinctive culture of Macao and prosperous economy accelerates the renewal of this ancient "Lotus Island". The Ruins of St. Paul's witnesses the changes of time, Grand Lisboa Macao lights up the night sky of this metropolis, and Amizade Bridge spans the ocean like a rainbow. In the lively fish market, Drunken Dragon Festival Performance inherits the unique folk customs of Macao. The enduring faith of Macao's people over the centuries finds its symbol in the majestic statue of Mazu which stands proudly along the expansive coastline.

Popular sports in Macao include traditional wushu and hockey.

大三巴牌坊

澳门的标志性建筑，其正式名称为圣保禄大教堂遗址，澳门八景之一，世界文化遗产。

Ruins of St. Paul's

The Ruins of St. Paul's is the landmark in Macao. It is one of the eight scenic spots in Macao and is a World Cultural Heritage Site.

澳门塔

澳门著名的大型旅游设施，标志性建筑，东南亚最高观光钢塔。

Macao Tower

The Macao Tower is a famous tourist attraction and landmark in Macao. It is the tallest sightseeing steel tower in Southeast Asia.

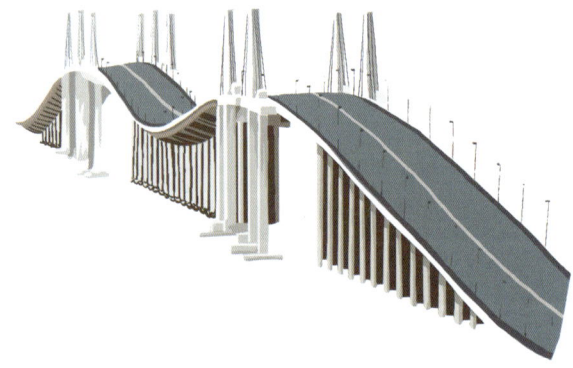

澳门友谊大桥

连接澳门半岛和氹仔岛的第二条跨海大桥，与澳氹大桥的夜景共同组成澳门八景之一的"镜海长虹"。

Amizade Bridge

The Amizade Bridge is the second sea-crossing bridge in Macao that connects the Macao Peninsula and Taipa Island. Together with the nightscape of the Macao-Taipa Bridge, it forms one of the "Long Rainbow across the Mirroring Sea" of the eight scenic spots in Macao.

新葡京酒店

酒店外形犹如一朵盛开的巨大莲花，是澳门的地标之一。

Grand Lisboa Macao

With the shape of a huge lotus in full bloom, the hotel is one of the landmarks in Macao.

东 亚 East Asia

鱼行醉龙节

澳门鲜鱼行独有的一项传统节庆活动，又称鱼行醉龙醒狮大会，是国家级非物质文化遗产之一。舞醉龙、舞醒狮是节日中两项主要的表演活动。

Drunken Dragon Festival Performance

Also known as the Drunken Dragon and Lion Dance Gala, Drunken Dragon Festival Performance is a unique folk festival celebrated by fishmongers in Macao and a national intangible cultural heritage. Drunken dragon dance and lion dance are two main performances in the festival.

妈祖阁

亦称"妈阁庙""天后庙"，简称"妈阁"，在澳门西南端妈阁街，为澳门历史最悠久的古刹。

Mazu Pavilion

Mazu Pavilion, also know as "Ma Pavilion Temple" and "Tin Hau Temple", abbreviated as "Ma Pavilion", is the oldest ancient temple in Macao at the southwestern end of Ma Pavilion Street.

莲花

澳门古称"莲岛"，区花为莲花，象征清廉、圣洁。

Lotus Flower

Lotus flower is the symbol of Macao, which was traditionally called the "Lotus Island". The lotus flower symbolizes incorruptibility and holiness.

葡式蛋挞

1989 年，英国人安德鲁·斯托将葡式蛋挞带到澳门，自此葡式蛋挞成为澳门著名小吃。

Portuguese-Style Egg Tart

In 1989, a British man called Andrew Stow brought Portuguese-style egg tart to Macao. Since then, egg tarts have become a popular snack in Macao.

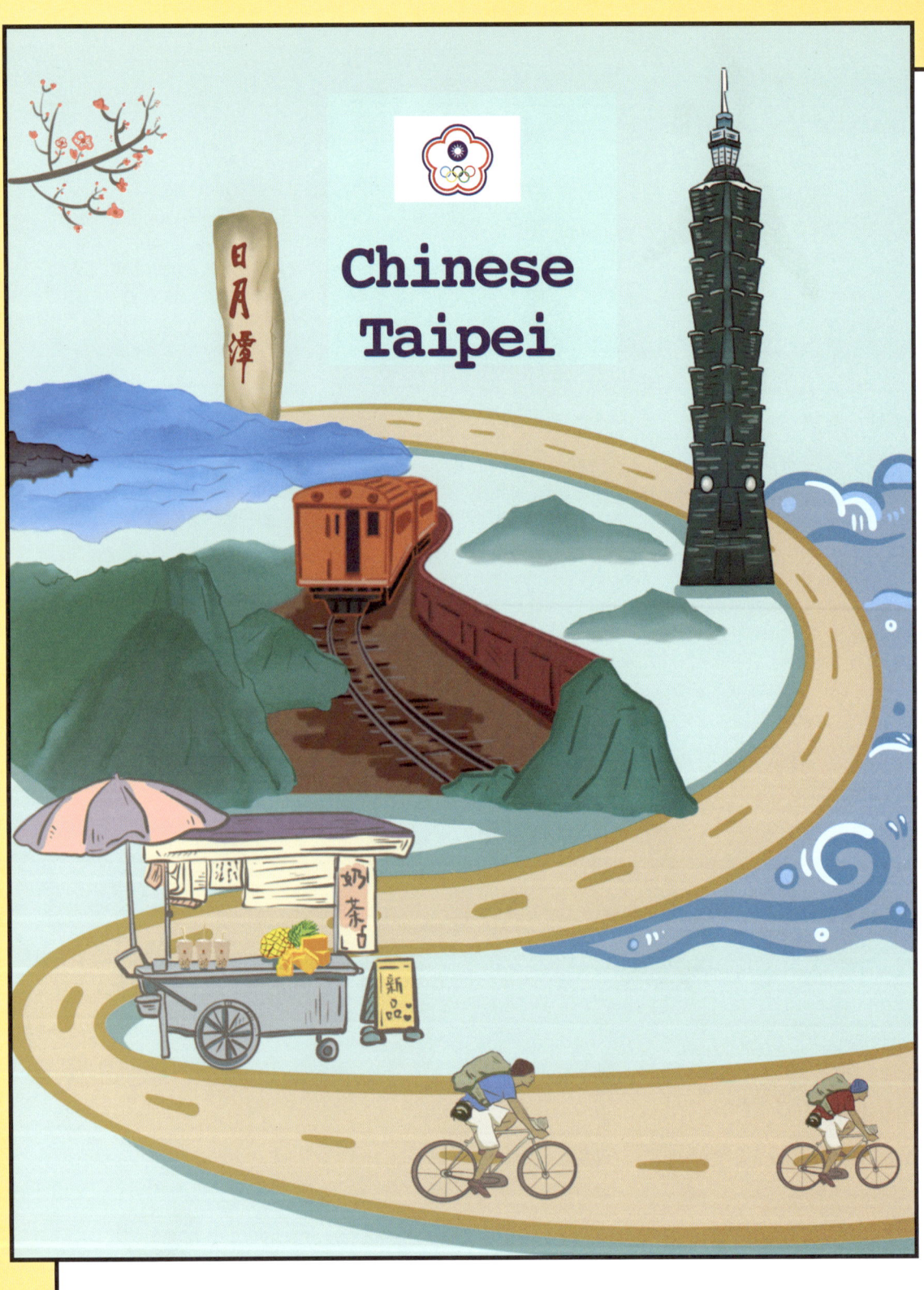

一分钟阅读

中国台北
Chinese Taipei

台湾是祖国宝岛，自古为中国领土不可分割的一部分，传承着古老的中华文化。阿里山和日月潭是台湾风光的象征，台北101大楼是台湾经济发展的重要标志。台湾夜市提供种类繁多又富地方特色的小吃，包括海蛎煎、珍珠奶茶、虾卷和刨冰等。

台湾流行的运动项目有网球、台球、棒球和跆拳道等。

Taiwan is the treasured island and an inseparable part of China since time immemorial, and inherits traditional Chinese culture. Ali Mountain and Sun Moon Lake are iconic scenes of Taiwan. The Taipei 101 is a significant symbol of the economic development of Taiwan. The night market offers a wide variety of local snacks, including fried oysters, bubble tea, shrimp rolls, shaved ice and so forth.

Popular sports in Taiwan are tennis, billiards, baseball and taekwondo, etc.

台北 101 大楼

原名台北国际金融中心，坐落于台北市信义区金融贸易区中心，高 508 米，2004 年竣工投用，造型设计上采用了竹子的意象，是当代建筑科技与中国传统文化融合的杰作。

Taipei 101

Formerly known as the Taipei World Financial Center, Taipei 101 is in the finance and trade center of Xinyi District, Taipei City. Opened in 2004 with a bamboo-look façade, this 508-meter-height skyscraper is a masterpiece combining traditional Chinese culture and modern architectural technique.

阿里山

坐落于嘉义市东部，山区气候温和、林木葱翠，是台湾著名旅游胜地。

Ali Mountain

Located in east Chiayi City, Ali Mountain is a treasure house with lush forests where the climate is moderate and mild. It is a renowned tourist attraction of Taiwan.

东 亚 East Asia

日月潭

　　台湾最大的天然淡水湖，清代即被选为台湾八大景之一。它以光华岛为界，北半湖形状如圆日，南半湖形状如弯月，日月潭因此得名。

Sun Moon Lake
As the largest natural freshwater lake in Taiwan, the Sun Moon Lake was listed in the eight scenes in Taiwan in the Qing Dynasty. The lake is separated by Lalu Island, with the northern part resembling the round sun and the southern part looking like the crescent moon.

凤梨酥

　　台湾风味点心，以低筋面粉等制面皮，以菠萝、冬瓜等制内馅。

Pineapple Tarts
Made of low gluten flour and pineapple jam or slices, the pineapple tart is a well-known Taiwanese snack.

珍珠奶茶

　　台湾颇具代表性的茶类饮料，由茶和牛奶制成饮品，再加入由木薯粉制成的"珍珠"而成。

Bubble Tea
The bubble tea is a representative tea-based drink of Taiwan, made of milk tea with tapioca pearls.

一分钟阅读

中国香港
Hong Kong, China

全称中华人民共和国香港特别行政区。香港包括香港岛、九龙、"新界",摩天大楼林立,汇聚东西方文化,彰显繁荣都市华彩。站在太平山顶,维多利亚湾的景色尽收眼底。香港体育馆常有大型比赛和表演,国际机场是香港繁华的象征,双层电车是香港别具一格的交通工具。香港是举世闻名的"东方之珠"和国际金融中心。

自行车、马拉松和赛马是香港较热门的运动项目。

Full name: the Hong Kong Special Administrative Region of the People's Republic of China. Hong Kong consists of Hong Kong Island, the Kowloon Peninsula, and the "New Territories". Bathing in both eastern and western culture, Hong Kong is a vibrant metropolis with numerous skyscrapers. From the top of the Victoria Peak, the enchanting sight of Victoria Harbor unfolds in a panoramic view. Hong Kong Coliseum regularly holds large-scale competitions and shows; Hong Kong International Airport stands for the prosperity of the metropolis; the tramway is a unique vehicle of Hong Kong. Famously known as the "Pearl of the Orient", Hong Kong stands as globally acclaimed hub for finance.

Cycling, marathon and horse racing are popular sports in Hong Kong.

维多利亚港

位于香港岛和九龙半岛之间的海港,世界三大天然良港之一。

Victoria Harbor

The Victoria Harbor sits between the Hong Kong Island and the Kowloon Peninsula, and is one of the world's three most important natural harbors.

香港体育馆

位于九龙红磡的比赛、演艺场馆,外形上宽下窄,像一颗钻石或一座倒金字塔,已有上百位明星在这里举办过演唱会。

Hong Kong Coliseum

Located in Hung Hom, Kowloon, Hongkong Coliseum is a multi-purpose arena for indoor competitions and performances. Its shape is wide at the top and narrow at the bottom, resembling a diamond or an inverted pyramid. The coliseum has held concerts of more than 100 stars.

香港国际机场

位于"新界"大屿山赤鱲角,为4F级民用国际机场,世界上非常繁忙的航空港之一。全球超百家航空公司在此运营。

Hong Kong International Airport

Located at Chek Lap Kok, Lantau Island in "New Territories", Hong Kong International Airport is a 4F international civil airport and one of the busiest airports in the world with more than 100 airlines operating there.

香港中环摩天轮

一座约60米高的巨型摩天轮,位于中环海滨长廊上。

Hong Kong Observation Wheel

Hong Kong Observation Wheel is a 60-meter-tall huge ferris wheel located at the Central Harborfront.

东 亚 East Asia

太平山

原名"硬头山",古称香炉峰,海拔 554 米,是香港岛的最高峰。

Victoria Peak
With its elevation of 554 meters, the Victoria Peak is the highest hill in Hong Kong.

山顶缆车

人们登太平山顶的主要交通工具,来往中环商业区和太平山之间,路轨依山势而建,最高坡度达 27 度,集交通和观光功能于一身,已有百年历史。

Peak Tram
The Peak Tram is the major transportation to reach the Victoria Peak. Running from the Central Bussiness District to the Victoria Peak, the railway is built on the hillside with the steepest angle of 27 degrees. It combines transportation and sightseeing functions. It has a century-old history.

电车

香港保留了路面电车系统,电车是香港历史悠久的交通工具之一。

Tramway
The tram system is one of Hong Kong's oldest vehicles of transport.

天星小轮

维多利亚港的渡海交通工具,与电车、太平山顶缆车齐名,已有百年历史。

Star Ferry
Star Ferry is a cross-sea transportation vehicle in Victoria Harbor. It has a century-old history and is as famous as the tramway and the Peak Tram.

东南亚 Southeast Asia

东帝汶
Timor-Leste

全称东帝汶民主共和国。东帝汶是位于东南亚努沙登加拉群岛最东端的岛国，2002年正式成立。这里多山、湖、泉，一派优美的田园风光。12种不同颜色的小巴在首都帝力的街头穿梭，是东帝汶重要的交通工具。东帝汶的经济以农牧业为主，盛产咖啡、橡胶、紫檀木等。石油与天然气推动了东帝汶的工业化。

2004年，东帝汶第一次派出代表团参加奥运会。当地民众喜爱的运动是足球。

Full name: Democratic Republic of Timor-Leste. Timor-Leste is an island country in Southeast Asia, occupying the easternmost part of the Lesser Sunda Islands. The country was established in 2002. The country is mountainous, rich in lakes and springs, forming a natural idyllic landscape. Minibuses of twelve different colors run through the streets in the capital city Dili, acting as important transport vehicles in Timor-Leste. Most Timorese make a living by farming. Coffee, rubber and padauk are main productions of Timor-Leste. Petroleum and natural gas accelerate the process of industrialization in Timor-Leste.

Timor-Leste has participated in the Olympic Games since 2004. Football is popular in Timor-Leste.

拉美劳山

拉美劳山是东帝汶最高的山,山顶上矗立着一尊圣母玛利亚的雕像,高 3 米。

Tatamailau

Also referred as Mount Ramelau, Tatamailau is the highest mountain in Timor-Leste. On the peak there is a 3-meter-high statue of Virgin Mary.

传统民居

一种用竹子和泥浆结合而成的茅草顶民居,当地人称之为"曼贝"。

Manbae

Manbaes are typical dwellings of the Mambai people in Timor-Leste. They are bamboo-and-mud-made houses with thatched roofs, and are called "Manbae" by the locals.

东南亚 Southeast Asia

小摊贩

街边摊贩出售的多是富有当地特色的小商品、水果和咖啡等。

Street Vendors
Street vendors normally sell Timorese specialty miscellaneous goods, fruits, and coffee.

咖啡

东帝汶盛产咖啡，咖啡是当地的主要经济作物之一。

Coffee
Timor-Leste is rich in coffee. Coffee is one of the main local cash crops.

小巴

帝力有 12 种不同颜色的小巴，根据其各自固定的行驶线路命名为 1—12。约 10 座的小巴是东帝汶各个城市中最重要的交通工具。

Minibus
There are minibuses of 12 different colors in Dili, numbered from 1 to 12 according to their fixed routes. The ten-seat minibus is an important vehicle of public transport that run through cities in Timor-Leste.

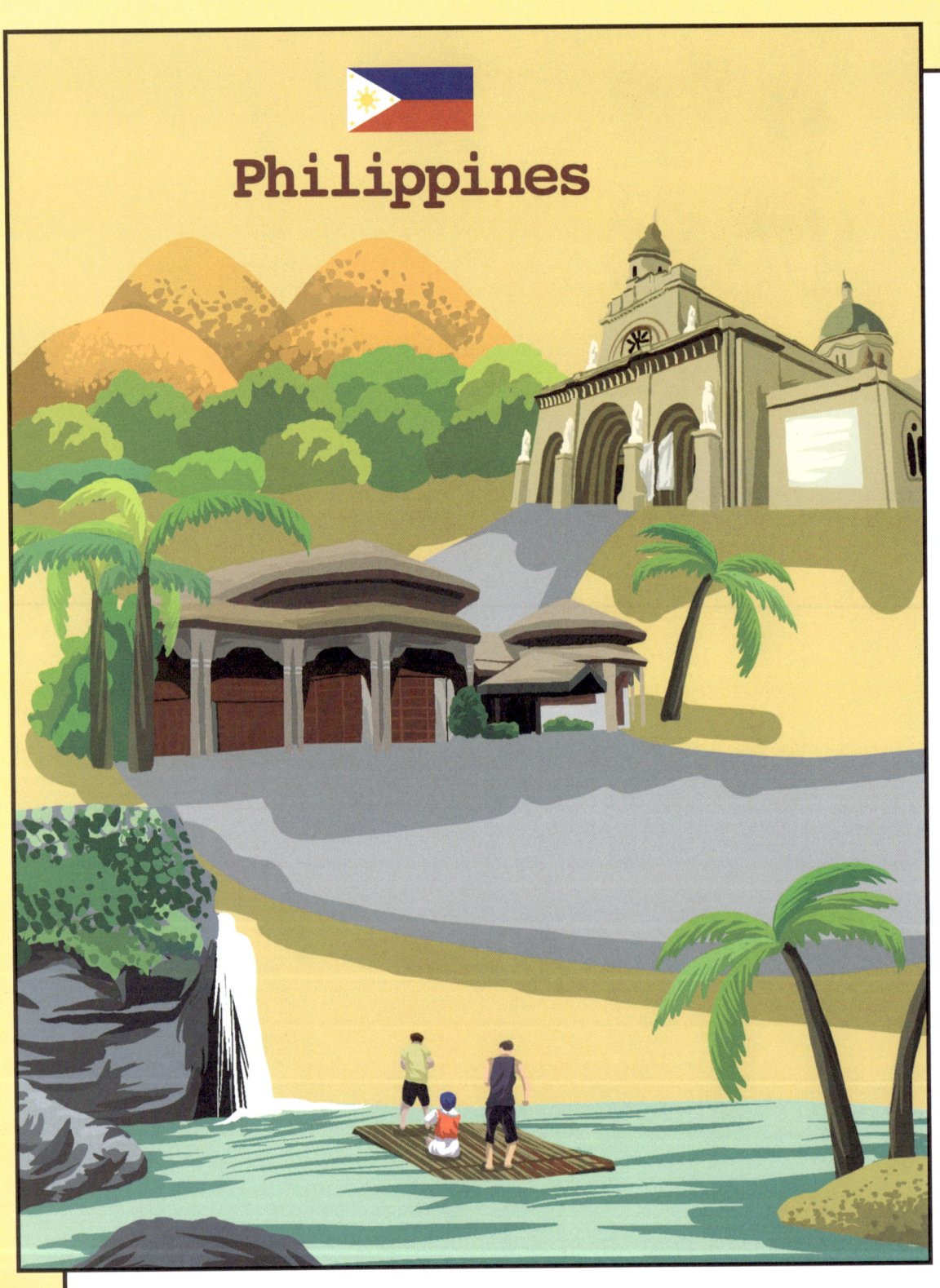

菲律宾
Philippines

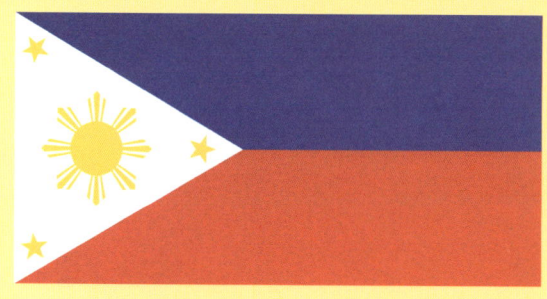

全称菲律宾共和国。菲律宾是西太平洋上的群岛国家，有"千岛之国"之称。东西方文化在这里相遇，首都马尼拉是菲律宾金融中心，充满现代化气息。椰子宫背靠马尼拉湾，马尼拉大教堂彰显罗马式建筑风采。山水叠秀凸显菲律宾美丽景色，巧克力山是闻名遐迩的自然奇景，白胜滩瀑布下竹筏激流荡漾，令人心旷神怡。

菲律宾热门的体育项目是篮球和拳击。马尼拉曾经举办第2届亚运会（1954）。

Full name: Republic of the Philippines. Known as the "Thousand Islands Country", the Philippines is an archipelago country in the Western Pacific. Eastern and Western cultures congregate here. The capital city Manila is the financial center of the Philippines and is full of modern charm. The Coconut Palace stands adjoining the Manila Bay. The Manila Cathedral manifests Romanesque architectural style. Mountains and waters jointly make up the impressive scenery of the Philippines. The Chocolate Hills are famous as a natural wonder, and under the Pagsanjan Falls, the sailing bamboo rafts are also a pleasant scenery.

Basketball and boxing are popular sports in the Philippines. Manila held the 2nd Asian Games in 1954.

椰子宫

位于菲律宾首都马尼拉市填海造地的新城区,是一座用椰子树建造的大厦,人称"椰子博物馆"。

Coconut Palace
Located on the land reclaimed from the sea in the new district of the capital city Manila, the Coconut Palace is a building made of materials from coconut trees, hence called the "gallery of coconut".

椰子树

菲律宾是椰子树的王国,椰子经济养活了菲律宾不少人口,椰子树在当地被尊称为"生命之树"。

Coconut Trees
The Philippines is also called the nation of coconuts. People in the Philippines treasure coconuts as the "tree of life", upon which lots of the nation make a living.

马尼拉大教堂

始建于1581年,是罗马式教堂建筑。

Manila Cathedral
Originally built in 1581, the Manila Cathedral is Romanesque architecture.

东南亚 Southeast Asia

巧克力山

位于菲律宾保和岛中部的一处自然奇景,由一千多座圆锥形小山丘组成。在雨季,草木是绿色的,但每到旱季,草木就会干枯,转为褐色,犹如一颗颗巧克力摆放在大地上,巧克力山因此得名。

Chocolate Hills
The Chocolate Hills, located in the middle of the Bohol Island, are fantastic natural sceneries. There are more than 1,000 conical hills which are covered with green grass that turns brown during the dry season, just like chocolate bars.

百胜滩

由大瀑布冲击而成,沿途九曲十八弯,急流险滩涌现不绝,两岸景色变化无穷。

Pagsanjan Gorge
The Pagsanjan Gorge, where the Pagsanjan Falls are located, is a narrow and verdant gorge with surging rapids and various natural sceneries.

泛舟人

百胜滩上,人们泛舟河上,沿途可看由岩壁和热带树木所构成的溪谷美景。喜爱冒险的年轻人会乘坐木筏穿过瀑布,感受那奔流直下、千军万马一般的瀑布冲击力。

Characters on Canoe
Along the Pagsanjan Gorge, visitors can enjoy the valley scenery of both cliffs and tropical plants on the canoes. Those who prefer adventures have the option to take the canoes through the curtain of the falls to feel the powerful cascading water heading downstream.

柬埔寨
Cambodia

全称柬埔寨王国。柬埔寨位于中南半岛南部，与越南、泰国、老挝毗邻。吴哥城的浮雕诉说着王朝历史和百姓生活，女王宫的山墙吟唱着印度教的史诗。湄公河、巴萨河、洞里萨河在金边交汇，洞里萨湖滋养了环湖城市。

柬埔寨的传统运动是高棉拳，现在流行的运动有篮球、足球、台球等。

Full name: the Kingdom of Cambodia. Cambodia is a country located in the Indochina Peninsula in Southeast Asia. It borders Viet Nam, Thailand and Laos. The stone carving of Angkor Wat tells the history of former empires and the life of ordinary people; the wall carvings of Banteay Srei sing Hinduist epics. The Mekong River, Bassac River and Tonle Sap River converge in the capital city Phnom Penh, alongside which the lake Tonle Sap nourishes cities around.

Khmer fist is a traditional Cambodian sport. Popular sports in Cambodia also include basketball, football, billiards, etc.

吴哥窟

建于12世纪，柬埔寨古代石构建筑和石刻浮雕的杰出代表。

Angkor Wat

Angkor Wat was built in the 12th century. It is an outstanding example of Cambodia's arcient stone architeture and stone carvings.

巴戎寺

位于吴哥地区，是一座佛教寺院。巴戎寺最著名的是刻在塔身的巨大的四面佛雕像，象征高棉王国的强盛。

Bayon Temple

The Bayon Temple is a Khmer Buddhist temple in the Angkor region in Cambodia. Its most distinctive feature is the multitude of serene and smiling stone faces associated with Buddha on the many towers, symbolizing the strength of the Khmer Kingdom.

洞里萨湖

又名"金边湖"，位于柬埔寨境内西部，中南半岛最大的淡水湖，也是柬埔寨人民的"生命之湖"。

Tonle Sap Lake

The Tonle Sap Lake, also known as Phnom Penh Lake, located in western Cambodia, is Indochina Peninsula's largest freshwater lake and the local's lake of life.

东南亚 Southeast Asia

金边王宫

　　一组金色屋顶、黄墙环绕的建筑，有大小宫殿二十多座，回廊上是仿吴哥窟的浮雕。这是柬埔寨国王居住、办公和会见外宾的地方。

Royal Palace of Cambodia
The Royal Palace of Cambodia is a complex of over twenty buildings which have golden roofs and yellow walls, served as a royal residence for living, working, and meeting with foreign visitors. The anaglyphs in the corridor are replicating those in Angkor Wat.

皇家舞剧

　　有一千多年的历史，以其优雅的手势和色彩艳丽的服饰著称。

Royal Dance
With over 1,000 years history, the Cambodiam royal dance features its elegant posture and colorful costume.

大皮影戏

　　又称"喃大皮"，柬埔寨非物质文化遗产，也是高棉戏剧中较为古老的门类，可追溯至1世纪，其特点是由整张皮革制作皮影道具。

Cambodian Shadow Puppetry
Also known as Sbaek Thom (nan large leather), shadow puppetry is an intangible cultural heritage of Cambodia. It is an older form of Cambodian drama, which can be dated back to the 1st century. The puppets are made from an entire piece of leather.

老 挝
Laos

全称老挝人民民主共和国。老挝是位于中南半岛北部的内陆国,森林面积广大,大象很多,素称"万象之邦"。首都万象在湄公河畔,散发着浓郁的佛教气息,凯旋门是老挝人民争取民族独立的标志。灵芝、石斛、古树茶是老挝优越的自然环境与人民辛勤劳作的见证。老挝泼水节热闹非凡,赛舟、花车、夜市展示了老挝人民美好生活的画卷。

老挝流行的运动有排球、足球和藤球等。

Full name: the Lao People's Democratic Republic. Laos is a landlocked country in the north Indochina Peninsula. With a thickly forested landscape and a large amount of elephants, it gets the nickname of "the Land of a Million Elephants". The capital city Vientiane flourishes alongside the Mekong River, full of rich Buddhistic atmosphere. The Patuxay symbolizes the struggle for independence of the Lao people. Reishi, caulis dendrobii and old tree tea are proofs of Laos' superior natural environment and the hard work of their people. Laos Water Festival is lively, boat racing, parades, and night markets all exhibit the beautiful Lao life.

The most popular sports in Laos are volleyball, football and sepaktakraw, etc.

凯旋门

位于万象市中心,其拱门基座上是典型的老挝寺庙雕刻。凯旋门为纪念战争中牺牲的人民而建,1975年,群众通过此门庆祝胜利,故称其为凯旋门。

Patuxay

Patuxay is located in the center of Vientiane. The small towers of the arch, with temple-like ornamentation, are designed in the Laotian style. It was built in memory of the Laotian soldiers who fell down during wars. In 1975, people gathered for the victory of revolution, parading and marching through the arch.

塔銮

老挝的佛教圣地,塔銮的全部建筑为灰砖结构,由 1 个主塔和 30 个卫星塔组成。

That Luang

That Luang is a sacred place of Buddhism in Laos. The main tower and 30 satellite towers were built with grey blocks.

香昆寺卧佛

老挝香昆寺有一座巨型卧佛,佛像眼睛微闭,单手侧枕,祥和地守护着身下的世界,卧佛前方林立着大大小小的雕像。

Reclining Buddha

The giant reclining Buddha of the Xieng Khuan Temple in Laos guards the world under him peacefully. Lying on one side, his eyes were closed. Large and small statues stand in front of the reclining Buddha.

东南亚 Southeast Asia

泼水节

又称宋干节,老挝的传统新年节日。每年4月中旬,人们相互泼水,祈求洗去过去一年的不顺,带来新一年的好运气。

The Water Festival

The Water Festival, also known as the Songkran Festival, is the traditional new year festival in Laos. It is held in middle April when people pour water to each other to wash out the setbacks happened last year and to hope for blessings and luck in the new year.

亚洲象

大象是老挝的吉祥物,随着森林被破坏,亚洲象数量急剧下降,目前已成濒危动物。

Asian elephant

Elephants are mascots in Laos. The sum of Asian elephants has dropped drastically as forests were being destructed. Now, Asian elephants are endangered in Laos.

古树茶

古树茶是指树龄在百年以上的树产的茶,在老挝北部丰沙里省有茶树群落,但数量稀少。

Old Tree Tea

In some parts of Laos, tea is made from tea trees over a hundred years old, which is called old tree tea. In Phongsaly in northern Laos, there are tea tree communities, but low in abundance.

灵芝

老挝属热带、亚热带季风气候,植被丰富,有很多野生灵芝,如竹灵芝。

Reishi

Laos is a tropical and subtropical monsoon climate region with rich vegetation, full of wild reishi, especially a species of reishi growing in bamboo forests.

马来西亚
Malaysia

马来西亚由马来半岛南部的西马和加里曼丹岛北部的东马两部分组成,自然资源丰富,海岛孕育了多民族和多元文化。国家清真寺可以体验用现代方式阐释的伊斯兰教传统艺术,在石油双塔之顶可以一览吉隆坡的繁华,京那巴鲁国家公园可以欣赏马来西亚多种多样的自然物种。

马来西亚是世界羽毛球强国之一,在各类国际赛事中多次获得奖牌。

Malaysia is separated by the South China Sea into two regions, Peninsular Malaysia and Kalimantan's East Malaysia. Malaysia is rich in natural resources. Islands breed Malaysia's ethnic diversity and diversed cultures. In the National Mosque of Malaysia, one can experience the modern interpretation of traditional Islamic arts. From the top of the Petronas Twin Towers, one can get a panoramic view of the prosperity of the capital city Kuala Lumpur. Kinabalu National Park offers a chance to enjoy massive natural species of Malaysia.

Malaysia has advantage in badminton and has won medals frequently in various international competitions.

国家清真寺

位于吉隆坡市中心，建于 20 世纪，为东南亚较大的清真寺。屋顶由 49 个圆拱组成，最大直径为 45 米，呈 18 条放射星芒状，代表马来西亚 13 个州和伊斯兰教五项功课。

National Mosque of Malaysia
Completed in 20th century, the National Mosque of Malaysia is a mosque in central Kuala Lumpur. As the larger mosque in Southeast Asia, its roof is composed of 49 domes. The largest dome is 45 meters in diameter and star-shaped with 18 radial starburst. The points represent Malaysia's 13 states and the five pillars of Islam.

石油双塔

世界最高的双塔楼，坐落于吉隆坡市中心，塔高 452 米，与吉隆坡塔同为马来西亚的知名地标。

Petronas Twin Towers
The Petronas Twin Towers are the tallest twin towers in the world. They are located at the center of Kuala Lumpur with a height of 452 meters. Together with the KL Tower, they stand as landmarks in Malaysia.

京那巴鲁国家公园

马来西亚沙巴州的名胜之一，世界自然遗产，是植物生态的聚集地。

Kinabalu National Park
Located on the west coast of Sabah, the Kinabalu National Park is a place famous for its scenery. It is a World Natural Heritage Site and important biological site.

东南亚 Southeast Asia

唐人街

又名茨厂街，是马来西亚吉隆坡市内非常富有华人气息的一片街区。

Chinatown
The Chinatown in Kuala Lumpur is called Petaling Street. It is a block which features rich Chinese culture.

吉隆坡塔

位于吉隆坡咖啡山上，马来西亚地标之一。塔身净高421米，建成时是世界第四通信高塔。

Kuala Lumpur Tower
Located on the Coffee Hill, the Kuala Lumpur Tower is a landmark in Malaysia with a height of 421 meters, which ranks the fourth highest communication tower in the world when completed.

红颈鸟翼凤蝶

马来西亚拥有上千种蝴蝶，其中红颈鸟翼凤蝶是马来西亚的国蝶。

Trogonoptera Brookiana
More than 1,000 species of butterflies have been recorded in Malaysia. The trogonoptera brookiana is the national butterfly of Malaysia.

兰花

马来西亚境内有8000多种花，仅兰花就有800多种。当地盛产兰花系列的香水，芳香持久。

Malaysian Orchid
More than 8,000 species of flower have been identified in Malaysia, including over 800 species of orchid. The country abounds with orchid-flavored perfume.

缅 甸
Myanmar

全称缅甸联邦共和国。缅甸位于中南半岛西部，佛塔寺庙林立，被誉为"佛塔之国"。曼德勒皇宫遵循缅甸传统设计风格，仰光大金塔是缅甸人尊崇的佛教圣地。蒲甘是缅甸著名的古城和世界遗产，这里的上空热气球飘浮。茵莱湖上单脚划船的渔夫保留了千百年来的捕鱼方式。夕阳下，人来人往的乌本桥勾勒出缅甸独特的落日美景。

缅甸流行足球、藤球、田径、举重、赛船等运动。

Full name: the Republic of the Union of Myanmar. Myanmar is located in the west of the Indochina Peninsula. With large amount of pagodas and temples, Myanmar is known as the "Land of Pagodas". The Mandalay Palace keeps traditional design of the Burmese royal palace. In Yangon, the Shwedagon Pagoda is revered as the Buddhist shrine by Burmese. Hot-air balloons float over Bagan, a famous ancient city and World Heritage Site. The one-legged fishermen on the Inle Lake retain centuries-old fishing methods. When the sun sets, the crowded U Bein Bridge forms the unique sunset scenery in Myanmar.

Myanmar's popular sports are football, sepaktakraw, athletics, weightlifting and boat racing, etc.

曼德勒皇宫

缅甸贡榜王朝的皇宫,红色和金色为主色调,宫内有104座宫殿,整个建筑为木结构建筑,墙外有护城河。

Mandalay Palace

As the royal palace of the Konbaung Dynasty in Myanmar, the Mandalay Palace has red-brick wall surrounded by a moat. Built of wood, the entire architecture accommodates 104 halls.

仰光大金塔

缅甸的国家象征,与婆罗浮屠和吴哥窟一起被称为东方艺术的瑰宝,是驰名世界的佛塔。它的形状像一个倒置的巨钟,塔的四周挂着许多金银铃铛,风吹铃响,声传四方。

Shwedagon Pagoda

It is the national symbol of Myanmar. Together with the Borobudur Temple and Angkor Wat, the Shwedagon Pagoda enjoys the reputation as the treasure of oriental art and is of world renown. It is shaped like an inverted giant bell with many gold and silver bells hanging around. When the wind blows the bells, their sound spreads far away.

东南亚 Southeast Asia

热气球

蒲甘是缅甸著名的旅游城市,最出名的旅游项目莫过于乘坐热气球看佛塔、日出。

Hot-air Balloon
Bagan is a famous tourist city in Myanmar. The most popular attraction there is to take a hot-air balloon and view the sunrise and pagodas.

乌本桥

在缅甸的阿马拉布拉古城境内,横跨东塔曼湖,是世界上最长的柚木桥,桥墩、桥梁、铺桥的木板用的是珍贵的柚木。

U Bein Bridge
The U Bein Bridge lies in the ancient city of Amarapura. This bridge sketches across the Taungthaman Lake, making it the longest teakwood bridge worldwide. The piers and bridge were constructed with precious teak.

茵莱湖渔夫

当地渔民捕鱼时,一只脚踩在船板上,另一只脚悬空荡桨,手里紧握鱼篓。拥有特殊捕鱼形象的渔民,也被人们称为"独脚船夫"。

Fishermen on Inle Lake
Local fishermen step on the oar with one foot and stand on the surface of the lake when they are fishing, with the fish cage held tightly in their hands. This special fishing method earns local fishermen the reputation of "the one-legged fishermen".

泰 国
Thailand

　　全称泰王国。泰国位于亚洲中南半岛中南部，拥有独特的风土人情和文化习俗。首都曼谷的古老寺庙与摩天大楼比邻而立，古典和现代交相辉映。曼谷大皇宫尽显传统暹罗建筑之精华，玉佛寺是泰国人心中的圣地，在大京都大厦顶可俯瞰曼谷市容。双条车是泰国街头一大特色，菠萝饭是广受人们喜爱的泰国菜。

　　泰国体育运动普及，泰拳深受民众喜爱。曼谷曾经举办第5届（1966）、第6届（1970）、第8届（1978）及第13届（1998）亚运会。

　　Full name: the Kingdom of Thailand. Located in the south-central part of the Indochina Peninsula in Asia, Thailand is known as a country that features unique local conditions and cultural costumes. Ancient temples stand alongside skyscrapers in the capital Bangkok, symbolizing the integration of antiquity and modernity. The Bangkok Grand Palace displays the essence of traditional Siamese architecture; the Wat Phra Kaew is regarded as the holy place by Thais; on the top of the MahaNakhon can overlook the cityscape of Bangkok. Songthaews are highlights on the streets of Thailand and pineapple rice is a widely-welcoming Thai dish.

　　Muay Thai is particularly popular in Thailand. The capital city Bangkok held the 5th (1966), 6th (1970), 8th (1978), and 13th (1998) Asian Games.

曼谷大皇宫

泰国王室的皇宫,紧临湄南河,是曼谷市中心的一处大规模古建筑群,也是泰国历代皇宫中规模最大、最有民族特色的皇宫。

Bangkok Grand Palace
Bangkok Grand Palace is the royal palace of the Thailand royal family. Closely adjoining the Chao Phraya River, it is a large-scale complex of ancient buildings in the center of Bangkok and stand as the largest and ethnically distinctive royal palace in Thailand's history.

玉佛寺

泰国著名佛寺,是泰国王室进行宗教活动的场所,因寺内供奉着玉佛而得名。

Wat Phra Kaew
Known for its house of the Emerald Buddha, Wat Phra Kaew is the place in which the royal family of Thailand holds religious events.

四面佛

在泰国,四面佛被认为是法力无边、掌握人间荣华富贵之神,其四面分别朝向东、南、西、北,供信众祈福。

Four-faced Buddha
In Thailand, the Four-faced Buddha is considered as the god with boundless power, who masters the prosperity and wealth of the world. Its four sides face the east, south, west and north respectively, so that believers can pray anywhere.

东南亚 Southeast Asia

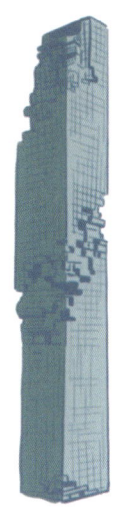

大京都大厦

首都曼谷新地标,是集住宿、娱乐、餐饮于一体的综合体。其因像素化的外观造型,被坊间称作"像素大厦"。

MahaNakhon
As the new landmark in the capital city Bangkok, MahaNakhon is a complex skyscraper which integrates accommodation, entertainment and catering. Its most distinguished feature is the pixelated appearance.

双条车

由皮卡车改造而成,在敞开式的车厢上安装一个遮阳棚,车厢两侧各安装一条长凳,就成了泰国的双条车。

Songthaew
A songthaew is adopted from a large truck, with an awning installed on the carriage and a bench on each side.

大象泼水

每年四月中旬是泰国的泼水节,泼水代表着清除邪恶,以美好迎接新的一年。在泰国,大象也向游客们喷水以庆祝一年一度的节日。

Elephants Spraying Water
The Songkran is in the middle of April each year. Splashing water denotes the eradication of evil and celebration of the new year. Elephants also spray water to tourists to celebrate the annual Songkran.

菠萝饭

泰国风味美食,以菠萝、米饭等食材制成的特色食物。

Pineapple Rice
The pineapple rice is a special delicacy of Thai flavor, it is cooked with pineapple, rice and other ingredients.

文 莱
Brunei

全称文莱达鲁萨兰国。文莱位于加里曼丹岛西北部，木板做成的水上房屋遍布文莱河两岸，传统的马来生活方式仍在水村延续。奥玛尔·阿里·赛福鼎清真寺矗立在斯里巴加湾，象征着文莱亘古不变的信仰。努洛伊曼皇宫的金顶在棕榈树间不断闪现，文莱人民的生活平和而安逸。

文莱流行的运动有桌球、高尔夫球、保龄球等。

Full name: Negara Brunei Darussalam. Brunei is located on the northwestern of Kalimantan Island. The wooden water dwelling spreads along the banks of Brunei River, passing on traditional Bruneian lifestyle. Standing on the bank reaching to the water, the Omar Ali Saifuddien Mosque in Bandar Seri Begawan symbolizes unchanged beliefs of this nation. The golden dome of the Istana Nurul Iman glitters in palm trees. The Bruneian people live in harmony on this peaceful land.

Billiards, golf, bowling, etc. are popular sports in Brunei.

奥玛尔·阿里·赛福鼎清真寺

文莱首都斯里巴加湾市的象征，是东南亚非常美丽的清真寺，建于1958年，以文莱第28任苏丹奥玛尔·阿里·赛福鼎三世的名字命名，纪念他的功绩。

Omar Ali Saifuddien Mosque

As a symbol of Bandar Seri Begawan, the capital city of Brunei, the Omar Ali Saifuddien Mosque is a very charming mosque in Southeast Asia. Completed in 1958, the mosque is named after Omar Ali Saifuddien III, the 28th Sultan of Brunei, to commemorate his contribution to the country.

杰米清真寺

当地人称为"国王的清真寺"，是文莱第29任苏丹建造的，又名"蓝色清真寺"。从外面看，带蓝色花纹的柱子高耸入云，圆顶由纯金打造，在阳光下熠熠生辉。

Jame' Asr Hassanal Bolkiah Mosque

Also called "mosque of emperor" by the locals, the Jame' Asr Hassanal Bolkiah Mosque was built by the 29th Sultan of Brunei. Its light blue minarets soar to the sky, which earn the mosque a nickname of the "blue mosque". The dome of the mosque, made of pure gold, gleams resplendently in the sunlight.

努洛伊曼皇宫

坐落于文莱河畔郁郁葱葱的山丘上，是文莱苏丹的住所，也是文莱政府的所在地。

Istana Nurul Iman

Located on a stretch of lush green hills to the Brunei River, the Istana Nurul Iman is the official residence of the Sultan of Brunei. It is also the seat of the Brunei government.

东南亚 Southeast Asia

高尔夫

文莱有各种各样的世界锦标赛级别的高尔夫球场。

Golf

There are many kinds of world championship level golf courses in Brunei.

文莱水村

水村是文莱人数百年来建在河上的居所,堪称"东方威尼斯",内部基本生活设施一应俱全,水村的主要交通工具为摩托艇。

Kampong Ayer

Kampong Ayer consists of a cluster of traditional villages built on the Brunei River for hundreds of years, known as "Venice of the East". These houses have all the necessary facilities for daily life. The main means of transportation in the villiage is motorboats.

棕榈树

文莱属热带雨林气候,生长着许多棕榈树。文莱的国徽中还有一根棕榈树干,象征着和平与希望。

Palm Tree

Brunei has a tropical rainforest climate with many palm trees. There is a palm tree in the national emblem of Brunei, symbolizing hope and peace.

一 分 钟 阅 读

新加坡
Singapore

全称新加坡共和国。新加坡是东南亚的一个岛国，濒临马六甲海峡。首都新加坡市以其整洁秀美的环境被誉为"花园城市"。新加坡河畔，鱼尾狮像是著名地标和国家象征，滨海艺术中心和滨海湾金沙酒店彰显现代大都市宏伟建筑的魅力。新加坡植物园是新加坡首个世界文化遗产，各种各样的热带植物在此生长。

新加坡曾经举办青奥会（2010）。流行的体育运动有足球、篮球、板球、橄榄球、游泳、羽毛球等。

Full name: Republic of Singapore. Bordering the Strait of Malacca, Singapore is an island country in Southeast Asia. The capital city Singapore is reputable as the "Garden City" for its neat and pretty environment. Along the Singapore River, the Merlion is a famed landmark and the national symbol. The Esplanade and Marina Bay Sands show the modern architectural charm of the metropolis. The Singapore Botanic Garden is Singapore's first World Cultural Heritage Site, where a wide variety of tropical plants thrive.

Singapore held the first Summer Youth Olympic Games in 2010. Popular sports in Singapore include football, basketball, cricket, rugby, swimming and badminton, etc.

滨海艺术中心

新加坡的标志性建筑,位于滨海区,主体宛如两颗榴莲,因而又名"榴莲艺术中心"。

Esplanade

Located in Marina Bay, the Esplanade is the iconic building in Singapore with appearance looking like two durians.

滨海湾金沙酒店

坐落于滨海湾,由三座大楼组成,楼内建有空中花园和游泳池。宾客们可以在游泳的同时,俯瞰新加坡的城市美景。

Marina Bay Sands

Composed of three connected buildings, this hotel is located in Marina Bay. There is a sky garden and swimming pool on the top, inviting guests to enjoy the cityscape while swimming.

鱼尾狮像

一种虚构的鱼身狮头动物,是新加坡的著名地标和国家象征。

Merlion

Merlion is the landmark and national icon of Singapore. The Merlion is a mythical creature with a lion's head and a body of fish.

东南亚 Southeast Asia

新加坡植物园

新加坡首个世界文化遗产，是热带岛屿植被繁茂的缩影。

Singapore Botanic Garden

As the first World Cultural Heritage Site of Singapore, Singapore Botanic Garden is the epitome of the lush vegetation of this tropical island.

胡姬花

即兰花，新加坡国花，也被称为"卓锦·万代兰"，寓意"卓越锦绣、万代不朽"。

Orchid

Orchid is the national flower of Singapore. It represents beauty, elegance and immortality.

肉骨茶

新加坡的特色美食。人们用猪排骨和中药包煲成汤，通常边吃排骨边饮茶汤。

Bak Kut Teh

Bak Kut Teh is a delicacy in Singapore. The soup is cooked with pork ribs and Chinese medicine, enabling people to drink soup while eating pork ribs.

虎牌啤酒

诞生于1932年，以绝佳的口味和上乘的品质赢得了多项国际奖项。

Tiger Beer

Launched in 1932, Tiger Beer has won multiple international prizes and awards for its great taste and superior quality.

印度尼西亚
Indonesia

全称印度尼西亚共和国。印度尼西亚位于亚洲东南部，地跨赤道，是世界上最大的群岛国家。首都雅加达是这个现代国家的中心，古城日惹是爪哇传统文化展示的窗口，胜地万隆是"万隆精神"的起源地。数百个民族的人民在此繁衍生息，各族文化蓬勃发展。木雕和巴迪布展现了印度尼西亚人虔诚的信仰和高超的手工艺，科莫多巨蜥见证了印度尼西亚优越的自然环境。

雅加达曾经举办第 4 届（1962）和第 18 届（2018）亚运会。印度尼西亚的传统体育项目有赛牛、独木舟等，现代体育强项是羽毛球。

Full name: Republic of Indonesia. As the world's largest island country, Indonesia is located in Southeast Asia, crossing the equator. The capital city Jakarta is the center of this modern country. The ancient city Yogyakarta is a living showcase of Javanese culture. The attractive city Bandung is the birthplace of "Bandung Spirit". Various ethnic communities live in Indonesia, evolving a colorful culture of diversity. Wood carving and batik show the craftsmanship and belief of Indonesian people; the Komodo dragon witnesses the great natural environment in Indonesia.

The capital city Jakarta held the 4th and 18th Asian Games in 1962 and 2018. Cow racing and canoeing, etc. are traditional sports of Indonesia. Its strength in modern sport is badminton.

亚非会议纪念博物馆

万隆市中心繁华的亚非大街旁有一栋乳白色三层建筑，原为荷兰人的高级俱乐部，印度尼西亚独立后被命名为独立大厦。亚非会议 25 周年之际，在大厦中建立了亚非会议纪念博物馆。

Asian-African Conference Museum

It's a three-story building located in the center of Bandung. After serving as an entertainment venue of the Dutch, it was renamed "Independence Building" after the independence of Indonesia. On the 25th anniversary of the Asian-African Conference, the Asian-African Conference Museum was inaugurated here.

婆罗浮屠

建于 8—9 世纪，意为"千佛坛"，是印度尼西亚佛教古建筑。

Borobudur

Borobudur is an ancient Buddhist buillding in Indonesia built around 8th to 9th century, meaning "Thousand Buddha Altar".

东南亚 Southeast Asia

赛牛

一项每年在水稻收获后举行的赶牛比赛，分旱地赛牛和水田赛牛，是印度尼西亚的传统体育项目。

Cow Racing

Cow racing is held after the rice harvest each year. Cow racing is divided into dryland racing and paddyfield racing. It is a traditional sport in Indonesia.

科莫多巨蜥

现存最大的蜥蜴类动物，又名"科莫多龙"。科莫多巨蜥为濒危的稀有动物，印度尼西亚已在科莫多岛上建立国家公园，以保护科莫多巨蜥的生存环境。

Komodo Dragon

It's also known as the Komodo monitor, the largest extant species of lizard. Komodo dragons are critically endangered. The Indonesian government has established national parks in Komodo to protect the environment for their survival.

巴迪布

一种蜡染印花布，其特点是布上印有色彩丰富的图案，如花卉、蝴蝶或几何图案等。

Batik

It is an Indonesian technique of waxresist dyeing applied to the whole cloth. Batik is featured with its colorful patterns including flowers, butterflies and geometric patterns.

木雕

印度尼西亚木雕一般采用檀木或者质地坚硬、花纹细密的雨树和柚木等木料手工雕凿，造型千姿百态。

Wood Carving

Wood carving, preferring hard and tense-patterned wood like teak, saman, and sandalwood, is of various designs and high craftsmanship.

一 分 钟 阅 读

越 南
Viet Nam

全称越南社会主义共和国。越南位于亚洲中南半岛东部。首都河内的巴亭广场开阔庄严，胡志明纪念堂雄伟肃穆。顺化皇城巍峨壮丽，下龙湾烟波浩渺。越南街头可以随处看到头戴斗笠、沿街叫卖的小贩，或是骑着摩托车呼啸而过的女子。深受欢迎的越南河粉，既是越南稻作文明的精彩缩影，也是一张走出国门的美食名片。

越南流行的体育项目有象棋、藤球、足球等。

Full name: the Socialist Republic of Viet Nam. Located in Southeast Asia, Viet Nam sits in the east of the Indochina Peninsula. In the capital city Hanoi, the Ba Dinh Square is capacious and solemn; the President Ho Chi Minh Mausoleum is majestic and dignified. The Imperial City in Hue is characteristic of magnificence and splendor; a wide expanse of misty water flows through the Ha Long Bay. On the streets, vendors wearing bamboo hats hawk along the streets while women on motorcycles whiz past. The popular pho is not only a microcosm of Vietnamese rice culture, but also a business card of food handed out abroad.

Vietnamese like chess, sepaktakraw, football, etc.

巴亭广场

位于首都河内市中心，是举行集会和节日活动的重要场所。

Ba Dinh Square
Located in the center of the capital city Hanoi, the Ba Dinh Square is an important place for assembly and festival activities.

顺化皇城

越南阮氏王朝的皇宫，位于古都顺化，是越南现存最大且较完整的古建筑群，1993 年被列入世界文化遗产名录。

Imperial City in Hue
The Imperial City in Hue is the royal palace of the Nguyen Dynasty and is located in the city of Hue. It is the largest and well-preserved historic architectures extant in Viet Nam. It was listed as a World Cultural Heritage List in 1993.

莲花

越南国花，是吉祥、平安、光明的象征。

Lotus
Lotus is the national flower of Viet Nam, symbolizing auspiciousness, safety, and brightness.

东南亚 Southeast Asia

下龙湾

越南广宁省的一个海湾，喀斯特地貌，为世界自然遗产，这里风光秀丽，闻名遐迩。

Ha Long Bay
Featuring thousands of karst limestones and attractive sceneries, the Ha Long Bay is a famous World Natural Heritage Site in Quang Ninh Province, Viet Nam.

越南河粉

越南享誉国际的经典美食。一碗正宗的越南河粉由汤底、河粉、肉和配菜组成。

Pho
Pho is a Viet Nam cuisine well-known all over the world. This soup dish consists of broth, rice noodles, meat, and vegetables.

越南春卷

以稻米磨浆制成的米皮包裹肉类或蔬菜，是风靡越南的一道美食。

Vietnamese Spring Roll
Vietnamese spring roll is one of the most popular dishes in Viet Nam. It is made with meat or vegetables wrapped in rice skin.

南 亚 South Asia

巴基斯坦
Pakistan

全称巴基斯坦伊斯兰共和国。巴基斯坦位于南亚次大陆西北部。河谷、沙滩、雪山，多样化的景观呈现出巴基斯坦独特的自然风光。位于首都伊斯兰堡的国家纪念碑象征巴基斯坦人民的无私奉献与团结精神，费萨尔清真寺静立在马尔格拉山下。拉合尔是巴基斯坦的历史名城，高耸的纪念塔是拉合尔的地标，沙利马尔花园是著名的古迹。

巴基斯坦流行的运动项目是板球、足球和曲棍球。

Full name: the Islamic Republic of Pakistan. Pakistan is located in the northwest of the Indian Subcontinent. Diversed landscapes of valleys, beaches and snow mountains exhibit the unique natural scenery of Pakistan. In the capital city Islamabad, the Pakistan Monument symbolizes the unity of the Pakistanis; the Faisal Mosque stands at the foot of the Margalla Hills. In Lahore, a historic city, the towering Minar-e-Pakistan is a landmark; the Shalimar Gardens is a famous antiquity.

Popular sports in Pakistan are cricket, football and hockey.

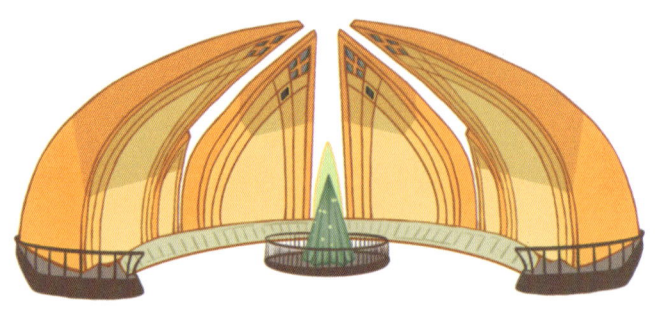

国家纪念碑

由四个大花瓣和三个小花瓣组成,正前方是一座五角尖碑。俯视时,正是巴基斯坦国旗的星月标志。

The Pakistan Monument

The monument is composed of four large petals and three small petals, with a pentagon obelisk sitting in front of it. Viewing from the top, the monument resembles the symbols of the star and the moon in the Pakistan national flag.

费萨尔清真寺

位于巴基斯坦首都伊斯兰堡,巴基斯坦最大的清真寺,是当地的标志性建筑。

The Faisal Mosque

Located in the capital Islamabad, the Faisal Mosque is the largest mosque in Pakistan. It is a local landmark.

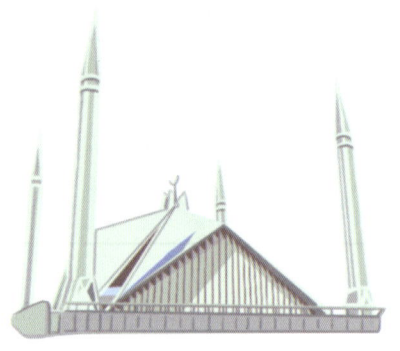

独立纪念塔

耸立在拉合尔古城旁的广场中央,塔座是朵白色的莲花,是巴基斯坦著名的纪念性建筑。

Minar-e-Pakistan

Minar-e-Pakistan is a famous monument in Pakistan. Standing in the center of the square adjoining the old city Lahore, the tower base is a white lotus.

真纳墓

巴基斯坦国父穆罕默德·阿里·真纳的陵墓,位于卡拉奇市中心,伊斯兰建筑风格。

Mazar-e-Quaid

Located in the center of Karachi City, the Islamic style mausoleum, Mazar-e-Quaid, is the resting place of Muhammad Ali Jinnah—the National Father of Pakistan.

南 亚 South Asia

沙利马尔花园

位于巴基斯坦文化古都拉合尔市郊，亭台楼阁围绕着一泓湖水而建，被称为"爱神之家"。

Shalimar Gardens
Situated on the outskirts of Lahore, a historical city of Pakistan, the pavilions are built around a lake, which earns Shalimar Gardens the reputation of the "House of Eros".

捻角山羊

巴基斯坦国兽，以一对卷曲的、螺旋形的大角著称。

Markhor
As the national animal of Pakistan, markhor is known for its curly and spiral large horns.

板球

巴基斯坦较强的运动之一。巴基斯坦板球队曾多次在各类国际赛事中取得好成绩。

Cricket
Cricket is one of Pakistan's strong sports. The Pakistan cricket team has achieved good results in various international competitions on many occasions.

素馨花

巴基斯坦国花。根据伊斯兰教教义，人们在公共场所必须散发出令人愉快的香气，因此芬芳的素馨花被奉为信仰的象征。

Frangipani
Frangipani is the national flower of Pakistan. According to Islamic doctrines, people must exude a pleasant fragrance in the public, therefore the balmy frangipani is regarded as a symbol of faith by the Pakistanis.

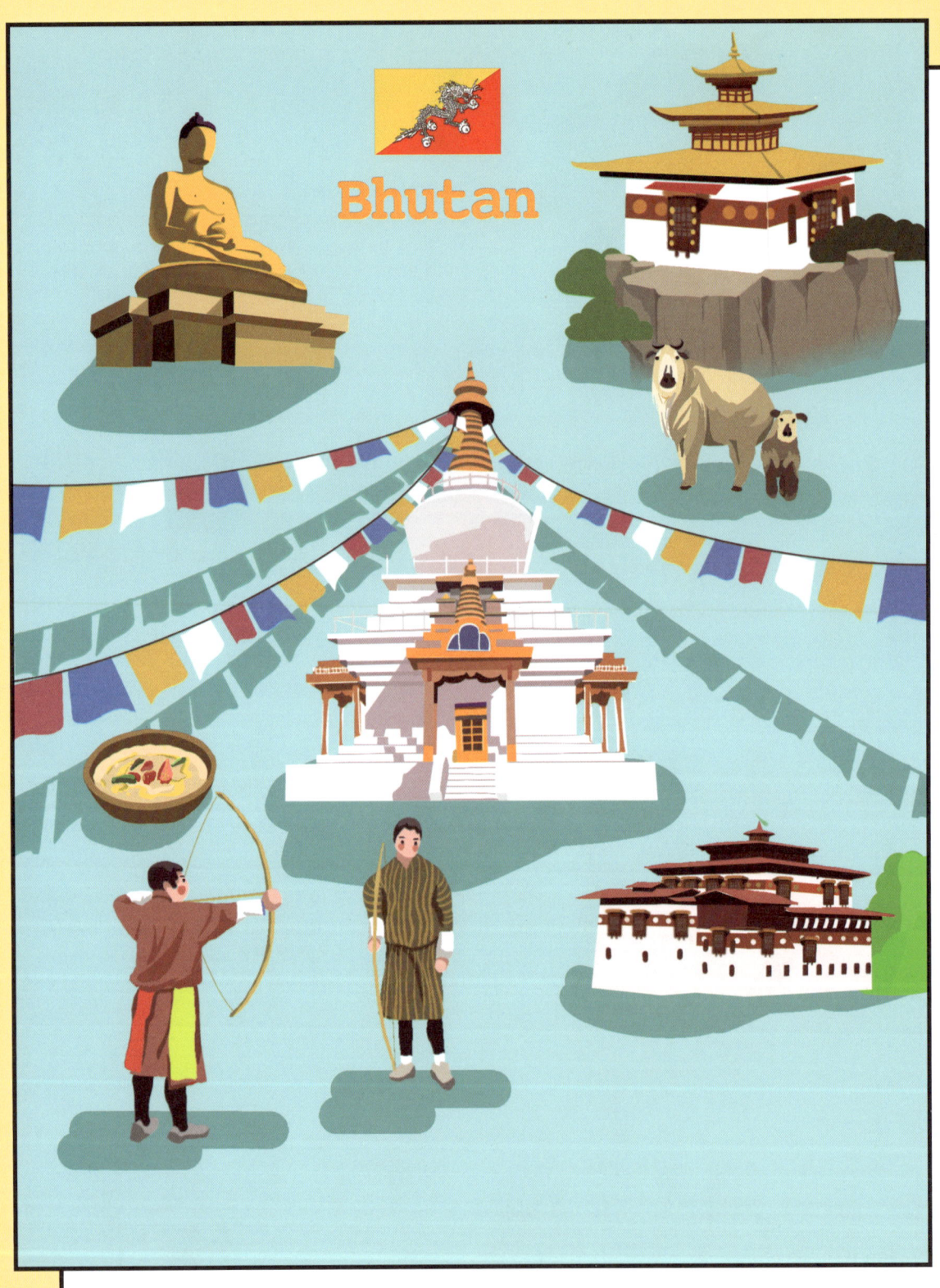

不 丹
Bhutan

全称不丹王国。不丹位于喜马拉雅山脉东段南坡，风景秀美而古朴。佛教精神在这里薪火相传，千年文化精心守护。国家纪念碑是首都廷布的重要地标，普那卡宗是不丹传统的宗教建筑，悬崖上的虎穴寺是不丹神圣的寺庙。

不丹的传统运动是射箭，不丹人民也喜爱篮球、足球等运动。

Full name: the Kingdom of Bhutan. Located on the southern slope of the eastern section of the Himalayas, Bhutan has beautiful and simple scenery. The Buddhism spirit is handed down through generations; thousand-year culture is carefully protected. National Memorial Chorten is the landmark of the capital Thimphu; Punakha Dzong is the typical religious architecture in Bhutan; Paro Taktsang on the cliff is a sacred temple.

The most well-known traditional sport in Bhutan is archery. Basketball and football, etc. are also popular in Bhutan.

国家纪念碑

为世界和平而建的纪念碑，是廷布人每日转经轮最集中的地方。

National Memorial Chorten

National Memorial Chorten is a monument to world peace. For people in Thimphu, this stupa is also the focus of their daily worship.

五彩经幡

不丹是一个宗教色彩很浓的国度，随处可见印着经文的五彩经幡，有蓝、白、红、绿、黄五种颜色。

Prayer Flag

Bhutan is a very religious country. Prayer flags with scriptures can be seen everywhere. Prayer flags are normally in five colors: blue, white, red, green and yellow.

普那卡宗

位于不丹父亲河和母亲河的交汇处，是不丹非常美丽的宗教城堡。

Punakha Dzong

Located at the confluence of the Po Chu River and Mo Chu River, Punakha Dzong is acknowledged as a very beautiful dzong in Bhutan.

大佛像

位于不丹首都廷布，高约 52 米，庄严地俯瞰着廷布风景。

Great Buddha Dordenma

Situated in the capital city Thimphu, the Great Buddha Dordenma is about 52 meters high, overlooking the scenery of Thimphu.

南 亚 South Asia

虎穴寺

坐落在帕罗山谷中 900 多米高的悬崖峭壁上，是不丹神圣的佛教寺庙。

Paro Taktsang

As a sacred Buddhist temple in Bhutan, the Paro Taktsang was constructed on the cliff more than 900 meters high in the Paro Valley.

射箭

不丹人最喜爱的体育休闲运动，被誉为不丹的国技。

Archery

Archery is the favorite sport of the Bhutanese and is renowned as the national sport of Bhutan.

塔金

不丹语，即羚牛，是不丹国兽，外形"六不像"，喜群居，是世界珍稀动物。

Takin

Takin is the national animal of Bhutan. This rare animal has a special appearance and likes to live in groups.

辣椒芝士

不丹的传统料理，国民美食，用辣椒和当地奶酪制成。

Emma Datshi

Emma Datshi is the traditional food and national dish of Bhutan. It is made from chili peppers and local cheese.

马尔代夫
Maldives

全称马尔代夫共和国。马尔代夫是印度洋上的群岛国家。阳光、沙滩、海洋是马尔代夫别具一格的名片。白沙铺成的道路上，马累星期五清真寺遥望海岸。湛蓝的海面上，雅致的水屋别具风格。人们依海而居，乘着传统的多尼船，饮着特制的淑女酒，生活质朴而宁静。

马尔代夫人喜爱沙滩排球，也喜爱羽毛球、板球、网球、乒乓球等运动。

Full name: the Republic of Maldives. Maldives is an archipelagic country in the Indian Ocean. Sunshine, beach, and sea form the unique picture of Maldives. On the white sand road, the Male Friday Mosque stares into the coast. On the clear sea, elegant water villas have a special flavor. With traditional dhoni boats to ride and the special wine Maldives Lady to taste, for Maldivians living by the sea, life is simple and peaceful.

Maldivians like beach volleyball, badminton, cricket, tennis, table tennis, etc.

星期五清真寺

马累的标志性建筑，是马尔代夫较古老的清真寺。

The Male Friday Mosque
The iconic architecture in Male. It is an old mosque in Maldives.

水屋

马尔代夫特色建筑，最初是岛上居民的住所，依靠钢筋或圆木柱植入海底而固定在水面上。

Water Villa
Water Villas are the characteristic buildings in Maldives. Originally used as the dwellings of island residents, water villas are fixed on the sea surface by relying on steels or round wood columns which go straight into the seabed.

特色海景

马尔代夫由千余个小珊瑚岛屿组成，最大的特色就是一岛一酒店，每个岛都有独特的韵味。

Unique Seascape
Maldives is composed of over a thousand small coral islands. The most remarkable feature of Maldives is one island with one hotel, and each island has its unique charm.

多尼船

马尔代夫传统船舶，两端像月牙一样高高翘起，整个船身呈弧形，用椰木做成。

Dhoni
Dhoni is a traditional boat of Maldives. With both ends raised like crescent, the hull is curved and made of coconut wood.

南 亚 South Asia

金枪鱼

马尔代夫附近的海域非常适合金枪鱼繁衍，马尔代夫是世界金枪鱼出口大国。

Tuna
Maldives is the home to tuna fish and the country is a large tuna exporter in the world.

淑女酒

一种调制鸡尾酒，不含酒精。

The Maldives Lady
The Maldives Lady is a specifically made cocktail without alcohol.

椰子树

早期马尔代夫人靠吃海鱼、喝椰汁繁衍生息，椰子树是马尔代夫人赖以生存的资源。

Coconut Plam
The Maldivians used to rely on sea fish and coconut milk to survive. Coconut palms are treasure trove and resources for Maldivians for survial.

传统服饰

休闲服是当地常见的服装。男子常穿白衬衣；女子服装色泽鲜艳，一般不戴面纱。

Traditional Clothes
Casual clothes are the most common garment. Men usually wear white shirts and women are brightly dressed and normally don't wear veils.

孟加拉国
Bangladesh

全称孟加拉人民共和国。孟加拉国是孟加拉湾畔秀丽的"水泽之乡"。稠密的河网为栖居此处的居民带来了生机与活力。繁忙的达卡市内，缤纷艳丽的三轮车熙熙攘攘。阿赫桑曼济勒粉红宫殿是达卡的一大地标，矗立的语言运动烈士纪念碑象征着孟加拉国人民为自由而斗争的民族精神。

孟加拉国人民最喜爱的体育项目是板球，卡巴迪是孟加拉国的传统运动。

Full name: the People's Republic of Bangladesh. On the shores of the Bay of Bengal, Bangladesh is a swampy scenic land. The dense river network bestows the Bengalese with vigor and vitality. Colorful tricycles bustle in the vibrant Dhaka City. Ahsan Manzil is a major landmark of Dhaka; the Shahid Minar symbolizes the national spirit of the Bengali people who fight for freedom.

The most popular sport in Bangladesh is cricket. Kabaddi is a traditional sport in Bangladesh.

阿赫桑曼济勒粉红宫殿

一座通体粉红色的宫殿,是首都达卡的地标之一。1872 年,一位地主在仓房的基础上将其改建成私邸,如今用作博物馆。

Ahsan Manzil

Ahsan Manzil is a pink palace and one of the landmarks of Dhaka. It was originally a private residence rebuilt by a landlord on the basis of a warehouse in 1872. Now it is a museum.

语言运动烈士纪念碑

孟加拉国国家文化的象征,为纪念 1952 年语言运动而建。

Shahid Minar

Shahid Minar was constructed to commemorate the Bengali Language Movement in 1952, the symbol of the national culture of Bangladesh.

拉尔巴格堡

位于孟加拉国首都达卡市中心,是一幢粉红色的建筑。

Lalbagh Fort

Located in the center of Dhaka City, the capital of Bangladesh, Lalbagh Fort is a pink buliding.

南 亚 South Asia

科克斯巴扎尔海滩

世界上较长的海滩之一，长 120 千米，是孟加拉国著名的旅游景点。

Cox's Bazar Sea Beach
As a popular tourist attractions in Bangladesh, the Cox's Bazar Sea Beach is one of the world's longest sea beaches with a length of 120 kilometers.

三轮车王国

孟加拉国以"三轮车王国"著称于世，三轮车是当地人短途出行最常用的交通工具。三轮车的车身和车棚上画有各种图案，最常见的为孟加拉虎。

Tricycle Kingdom
Tricycle is the most common transportation for locals to travel for a short distance and Bangladesh is known as "the Kingdom of Tricycle". Various patterns are painted on the body and carport of it, while the most common one is the Bengal tiger.

鹊鸲

孟加拉国国鸟，喜鸣叫，性格活泼好动，觅食时常摆尾。

Oriental Magpie-robin
The oriental magpie-robin, the national bird of Bangladesh and a famous songbird, is very lively and often wags its tail when foraging.

尼泊尔
Nepal

全称尼泊尔联邦民主共和国。尼泊尔位于喜马拉雅山南麓,拥有古老的宗教文化和众多佛塔庙宇,神像与市民相伴,寺院和店铺为邻。博达哈大佛塔声名远扬,各种宫殿寺庙展示了尼泊尔古典建筑之华美。精巧的手工艺在尼泊尔代代相传,提线木偶是尼泊尔的特色工艺品。

尼泊尔流行的运动是板球和足球。

Full name: the Federal Democratic Republic of Nepal. Nepal lies in the southern foothills of the Himalayas. This is a country with ancient religions culture and numerous pagodas, and a place where residents are accompanied by statues and shops are neighbored to temples. The largest round stupa in Nepal, Boudhanath, is world renowned. Various palaces and temples display the beauty of classic Nepalese architecture. Exquisite craftsmanship is passed on through generations; puppet is a handicraft of Nepalese characteristics.

Popular sports in Nepal are cricket and football.

博达哈大佛塔

世界文化遗产，据称是世界最大的圆佛塔。

Boudhanath Stupa

Boudhanath Stupa is a World Cultural Heritage Site and the largest round stupa in the world.

尼亚塔波拉庙

尼泊尔古迹，又称"五层塔"，塔内供奉着希提拉克希米女神。

Nyatapola Temple

The monument in Nepal, the Nyatapola Temple, also known as the five-story tower, enshrines Siddhi Lakshmi.

克里希纳庙

尼泊尔古迹，位于古都帕坦，被誉为"尼泊尔建筑艺术的奇迹"。除塔顶外，全部用石头建造。

Krishna Mandir Temple

Lying in the old city Patan, the temple is a historical site in Nepal and it owns the reputation of "the miracle of Nepalese architectural art". Except for the top part, the temple was completely built of stone.

南 亚 South Asia

高山雪峰

尼泊尔境内有数百座山峰，多数山峰被白雪覆盖，因此被称为"雪山之国"。

Mountains and Snowy Peaks
Nepal has hundreds of peaks which are covered in snow. Nepal is therefore known as "the country of snow mountains".

独角犀牛

在尼泊尔被视为国宝。尼泊尔南部的皇家奇特旺国家公园里生活着许多独角犀牛。

One-horned Rhinoceros
One-horned rhinoceros are regarded as the national treasure by Nepal. The Royal Chitwan National Park in south Nepal is the habitat of many one-horned rhinoceros.

双面提线木偶

尼泊尔的特色手工艺品，一种木偶戏的道具。

Double-sided Puppet
Double-sided puppet is a handicraft with Nepalese characteristics and the prop for puppet shows.

馍馍

尼泊尔最受欢迎的小吃，外形似中国的小笼包、饺子或烧卖。

Mo Mo
As the most popular snack in Nepal, mo mo has three forms, which are similar to small steamed bun, dumpling or shumai respectively.

斯里兰卡
Sri Lanka

全称斯里兰卡民主社会主义共和国。斯里兰卡是印度洋上一块洋溢着独特民族风情的"乐土",这里文化不衰,古迹犹存。佛牙寺以佛教圣地之称而闻名,狮子岩融人工奇迹与自然奇景为一体,加勒城堡的灯塔驻守海岸。古老的国度里,传统民俗代代相传。康提舞是僧伽罗舞蹈的代表,高跷海钓是斯里兰卡特有的风景,红茶将斯里兰卡之名传遍世界。

斯里兰卡流行板球、排球、网球和橄榄球运动。

Full name: the Democratic Socialist Republic of Sri Lanka. In the Indian Ocean, Sri Lanka keeps unique ethnic customs. In this "paradise", culture thrives and relics remain. The Temple of the Tooth is known as the holy place of Buddhism; Sigiriya integrates man made and natural wonders; the watchtower of the Galle Fort safeguards the coast. Traditional customs are shared through generations in this ancient land. Kandy dance is the representative of Sinhala dance; stilt fishing constitutes an exclusive scenery; black tea spreads the name of Sri Lanka to the world.

The famous sports in Sri Lanka are cricket, volleyball, tennis and rugby.

佛牙寺

斯里兰卡著名的佛寺，位于康提湖畔，又称"达拉达·马利戛瓦"，以供奉国宝释迦牟尼的牙舍利而闻名。

Temple of the Tooth

The Temple of the Tooth is a famous Buddhist temple on the shore of the Kandy Lake. Also called as Dalada Maligawa, it is renowned for enshrining the tooth relic of Sakyamuni, the national treasure of Sri Lanka.

鲁梵维利萨亚佛塔

位于斯里兰卡的阿努拉德普勒古城，是全世界佛教徒的朝圣之地。

Ruwanwelisaya Stupa

The stupa is in the ancient city of Anuradhapura, Sri Lanka. It is a place of pilgrimage for Buddhists all over the world.

狮子岩

斯里兰卡锡吉里耶城的一座构筑在橘红色巨岩上的空中宫殿，是斯里兰卡国宝级景点之一。

Sigiriya

Sigiriya is an aerial palace built on a large red rock in Sigiriya City. It is one of the most visited historic sites in Sri Lanka.

加勒城堡灯塔

位于斯里兰卡西南部，面向大海，是加勒城堡的标志性建筑。

Watchtower of the Galle Fort

Located in the southwest of Sri Lanka, the watchtower on the shore is the iconic architecture of the Galle Fort.

南 亚 South Asia

九拱桥

位于斯里兰卡的德莫达拉,被称为"天空之桥",由砖石和水泥建成。

Nine Arches Bridge

The Nine Arches Bridge in the town of Demodara is known as "the Sky Bridge". The bridge was made of masonry and cement.

高跷海钓

斯里兰卡一种古老的捕鱼方式,渔民们坐于高跷之上垂钓,号称世界上最奇特的捕鱼方式。

Stilt Fishing

Stilt Fishing is a traditional fishing method of Sri Lanka. With fishermen sitting on stilts, it is regarded as the most unique fishing method in the world.

锡兰红茶

出产于斯里兰卡,是一种统称(锡兰是斯里兰卡共和国的旧称)。

Ceylon Black Tea

Produced in Sri Lanka, Ceylon black tea is a collective name (Ceylon is what Sri Lanka used to be called).

薄煎饼

一种碗状薄饼,斯里兰卡的传统早餐,用米浆、椰子奶、椰子水和少量糖做成。

Egg Hopper

Egg hopper is a bowl-shaped pancake, traditional breakfast of Sri Lanka. Egg hoppers are made with rice milk, coconut milk, coconut water and a small amount of sugar.

印 度
India

全称印度共和国。印度是南亚次大陆最大的国家，古老的恒河和印度河润泽了这方水土。在这里，古印度文明千年传承，多民族文化交相辉映。印度名胜古迹众多，泰姬陵闻名遐迩，印度门依海而立，德里红堡是古代帝国繁荣昌盛的象征。飞饼是印度闻名世界的美食。

印度新德里曾经举办第1届（1951）和第9届（1982）亚运会。印度的传统体育项目有可可、卡巴迪、竿上技巧、绳上舞蹈等。

Full name: the Republic of India. India is the largest country in the South Asian subcontinent. The venerable Ganges and the Indus River nourish the country. For thousands of years, the ancient Indian civilization passes on in a country where multiethnic cultures complement each other. India enjoys a huge amount of scenic spots and historical sites: the Taj Mahal enjoys widespread reputation; the Gateway of India stands at the waterfront; the Red Fort witnessed the prosperity of the ancient empire. Roti prata is a world-famous Indian cuisine.

New Delhi, the capital of India, held the 1st Asian Games in 1951 and the 9th in 1982. Kho-kho, kabaddi, pole skills and rope dance, etc. are traditional Indian sports.

泰姬陵

莫卧儿王朝皇帝沙贾汗为纪念其妃子而建,是一座用白色大理石建成的巨大陵墓。

Taj Mahal
Built by the Mughal emperor Shah Jahan in honor of his concubine, the Taj Mahal is an ivory-white marble mausoleum.

印度门

一座兼有印度教和伊斯兰教建筑特色的拱门,为纪念英国国王乔治五世 1911 年访印而建。

Gateway of India
The Gateway of India was built with the features of both Hindu and Islamic style to commemorate the visit of King George V in 1911.

德里红堡

莫卧儿王朝建造的皇宫,属于典型的伊斯兰文化建筑,因整个建筑主体呈红褐色而得名。

Red Fort
The Red Fort is a historic fort that served as the main residence of the Mughal emperors, exemplifying the Islamic architecture. It is named for its massive enclosing walls of red sandstones.

南 亚 South Asia

恒河

恒河被印度人民尊称为"圣河"和"印度的母亲",恒河流域是印度文明的发源地之一。

Ganges
The Ganges is honored as "the sacred river" and "the mother of India" by Indian people and is considered as one of the birthplaces of the Indian civilization.

大象

在印度,大象是一种颇受尊重的动物,是强壮、长寿、聪明的象征,各种节庆活动中都会出现大象的身影。

Indian Elephant
In India, elephants are treated with respect. Frequently seen in various ceremonies and activities, elephants symbolize strength, longevity and wisdom.

印度飞饼

印度的特色风味美食,是用调和好的面粉在空中用"飞"的绝技做成,具有美味可口、浓郁香酥的特点。

Roti Prata
Roti prata is prepared by flipping the dough into a large thin layer. It is an Indian flatbread dish of good taste and rich flavor.

脆球饼

印度街头非常受欢迎的国民小吃,在油炸过后的酥皮球内放上土豆泥等馅料,加以酱汁制成。

Panipuri
Panipuri is one of the popular street foods in India. It is made of puff-pastry balls, in which filled with mashed potatoes and sauce.

中 亚 Central Asia

哈萨克斯坦
Kazakhstan

全称哈萨克斯坦共和国。哈萨克斯坦位于中亚，是世界上最大的内陆国。巴尔喀什湖碧波荡漾，郁金香四季盛开。独立纪念碑在阿拉木图共和国广场矗立，阿斯塔纳国际金融中心见证了首都的现代化发展。阿拉木图的麦迪奥雪山有着世界上著名的高山冬季运动综合体，让人们尽情体验滑雪的乐趣。

哈萨克斯坦是中亚的体育强国，拳击、自由式摔跤是其强项。

Full name: the Republic of Kazakhstan. As the largest interior country in the world, Kazakhstan is located in Central Asia. The Lake Balkhash ripples, tulips bloom all year round. The Independence Monument stands on the Republic Square in Almaty. The Astana International Financial Center represents the modernity of the capital. Located in the Medeu Valley in Almaty, the Medeu is a famous high-altitude winter sports complex in the world, inviting people to enjoy skiing.

Kazakhstan is a major sports country in Central Asia. Its famous sports include boxing and freestyle wrestling.

独立纪念碑

位于阿拉木图共和国广场，高 28 米，顶端有一位武士站在一头有翅膀的雪豹身上。

Independence Monument

Located on the Republic Square in Almaty, the monument is 28 meters high, with a golden warrior standing on a winged snow leopard on the top.

阿斯塔纳国际金融中心

2018 年 7 月 5 日建成，是连接中亚、高加索、东亚、中东和欧洲等经济体的重要金融中心。

Astana International Financial Center

Launched on July 5, 2018, Astana International Financial Center is a major financial center for the countries of Central Asia, the Caucasus, East Asia, Middle East and Europe.

可汗沙特尔

位于首都阿斯塔纳，被视作世界最大帐篷，内有许多商店和娱乐设施。其建筑设计是为了唤起人们对蒙古包的回忆。

Khan Shatyr

Known as the biggest tent in the world, Khan Shatyr is located in the capital city Astana. Under the tent is the shopping and entertainment venue. The design of the tent is to remind people of the yurt.

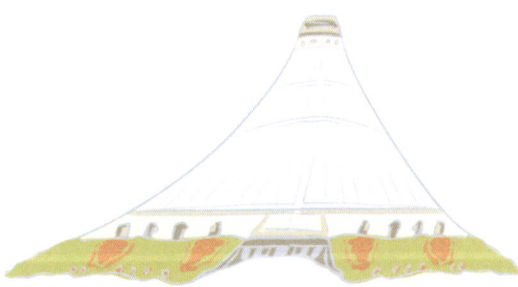

中 亚 CENTRAL ASIA

麦迪奥

位于阿拉木图，终年积雪不化，有着世界著名的高山冬季运动综合体，是哈萨克斯坦重要的冰雪运动训练基地和冰雪旅游中心。

Medeu

The Medeu Valley in Almaty, where the snow is persistent all year, has the famous high-altitude winter sports complex in the world, and is an important ice and snow sports center for training and sightseeing.

郁金香

哈萨克斯坦国花。境内四季均有郁金香盛开。

Tulip

Tulip, the national flower of Kazakhstan, blooms all year round.

金雕

哈萨克斯坦国鸟，象征着哈萨克斯坦人民的自由和豪放。

Golden Eagle

Golden Eagle, the national bird of Kazakhstan, is an emblem of the free and vigorous of the people of Kazakhstan.

吉尔吉斯斯坦
Kyrgyzstan

　　全称吉尔吉斯共和国。吉尔吉斯斯坦位于中亚东北部。天山山脉北麓的伊塞克湖位于群山掩映之中，湖水清澈，素有"上帝遗落的明珠"之称。比什凯克阿拉图广场的雕像玛纳斯是吉尔吉斯斯坦人民引以为傲的民族英雄，很多社团、街道、剧院、学校都以"玛纳斯"命名。吉尔吉斯斯坦的传统乐器表演颇具感染力，时而气势恢宏，时而温润优雅。

　　吉尔吉斯斯坦流行的运动项目有自由式和古典式摔跤等。

　　Full name: Kyrgyz Republic. Kyrgyzstan is located in the northeastern part of Central Asia. The Issyk-Kul Lake is in the Northern Tian Shan mountains. Surrounded by peaks, it owns the reputation as "the Pearl left by God". A statue of Manas stands proudly on the Ala-Too Square in Bishkek. Manas is a Kyrgyzstan national hero, whose name is often used to name associations, streets, theaters and schools. Traditional Kyrgyzstan music is full of enchantment, sometimes magnificent and sometimes serene.

　　Freestyle and Greco-Roman wrestling, etc. are popular in Kyrgyzstan.

伊塞克湖

高山不冻湖。当地有一句脍炙人口的谚语——"没到过伊塞克湖，就不算到过吉尔吉斯斯坦。"

Issyk-Kul Lake

The Issyk-Kul Lake is a high-mountain lake that never freezes. There is a saying in Kyrgyzstan, "Not until you went to the Issyk-Kul Lake could you say that you have been to Kyrgyzstan."

玛纳斯雕像

位于比什凯克阿拉图广场。玛纳斯是吉尔吉斯斯坦人民引以为傲的民族英雄。

Statue of Manas

Standing on the Ala-Too Square in Bishkek, the statue is named after Manas, the honored national hero in the heart of the people of Kyrgyzstan.

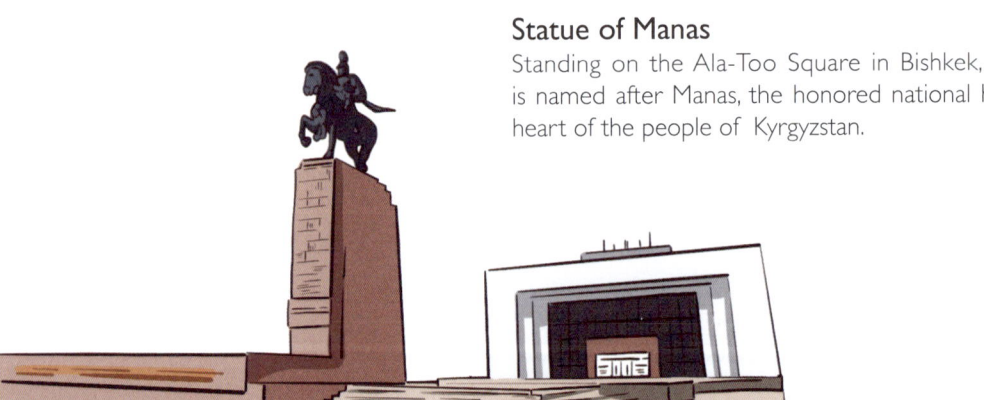

中 亚 Central Asia

布拉纳塔

又译诗歌塔，是吉尔吉斯斯坦托克马克市的历史纪念碑建筑，建于10—11世纪。

Burana Tower
Also translated as the Poetry Tower, the Burana Tower is a historical monument in the town of Tokmok. It is built between the 10th and 11th century.

最高会议大厦

位于首都比什凯克，是集总统府和议会办公地于一体的政府大楼。

Supreme Council Building
Located in the capital city Bishkek, the Supreme Council Building is a governmental building used as both the presidential palace and the parliament house.

库姆孜

一种三弦弹拨乐器，长约一米，琴杆细长，琴身一般用松木或杏木制作，琴箱近似梨形。库姆孜的演奏形式多样，有独奏、伴奏、合奏等，其音域宽阔，音色干净，具有生动的艺术表现力。

Komuz
Komuz is a three-stringed plucked instrument about one meter long, with a long and slender stem. The body is generally made of pine or apricot, and the case is approximately pear-shaped. Komuz can be played in various forms, including solo, accompaniments, ensembles, etc. It has wide range, clean tone, and colorful artistic expression.

塔吉克斯坦
Tajikistan

　　全称塔吉克斯坦共和国。塔吉克斯坦位于中亚东南部。塔吉克民族之父索莫尼的雕像矗立在杜尚别市中心。苦盏是一座古城，城中保存着中世纪的城堡和清真寺。一年一度的全国赛马比赛，是欢庆纳乌鲁斯节的项目。塔吉克人钟爱传统茶道，日常生活离不开品茶和吃美味的点心。

　　塔吉克斯坦流行的运动是山地自行车、登山、滑雪、足球等。

　　Full name: the Republic of Tajikistan. Tajikistan lies in the southeastern part of Central Asia. In the center of the capital Dushanbe rises the statue of Ismail Somoni, the father of the Tajik nation. Khujand is an ancient city where medieval castles and mosques stand. The national annual horse racing is an important part of the festival Nawrooz celebration. Tajiks cherish traditional tea ceremony. Their daily life is inseparable from tasting tea and eating delicious snacks.

　　Mountain biking, mountain climbing, skiing and football, etc. are popular in Tajikistan.

索莫尼雕像

位于首都杜尚别索莫尼广场。索莫尼是塔吉克民族之父,塔吉克有一种货币也以索莫尼命名。

Statue of Ismail Somoni

The statue is located on the Somoni Square in the capital city Dushanbe. Ismail Somoni, considered as the father of the Tajik nation, is also the man that a currency of Tajikistan is named after.

苦盏清真寺广场

坐落于苦盏市中心。苦盏是塔吉克斯坦第二大城市,中亚著名的古城之一。清真寺广场上有一群鸽子以及玩耍的孩子们。

Panshambe Bazaar Square

The Panshambe Bazaar Square is located in the center of Khujand, which is the second largest city in Tajikistan and one of the famous historic cities in Central Asia. There are a herd of pigeons flying and running children having fun on the square.

中 亚 Central Asia

国徽纪念碑

位于首都杜尚别，建筑顶部是塔吉克斯坦的国徽。

Stele with the Emblem of Tajikistan
Standing in the capital city Dushanbe, the Stele with the Emblem of Tajikistan has the national emblem on the top.

传统茶道

由瓷碗、茶壶、芳香的绿茶和美味的甜点组成，深受塔吉克人喜爱。

Traditional Tea Ceremony
Consisting of the ceramic bowl, teapot, fragrant green tea, and tasty desserts, the traditional tea ceremony is popular among the Tajik people.

赛马

为庆祝当地传统节日——纳乌鲁斯节而举办的传统文体娱乐活动之一。

Horse Racing
Horse racing is one of the traditional sports and cultural events be held to celebrate the local traditional festival Nawrooz.

土库曼斯坦
Turkmenistan

　　土库曼斯坦位于中亚西南部，拥有丰富的矿产资源。中立纪念碑象征着人民对和平和安全的向往，库尼亚-乌尔根奇的历史遗迹展示着民族建筑和手工艺的卓越成就，也见证着曾经的美丽城市。阿哈尔捷金马以速度和耐力著称，是世界现存最古老的马种之一，被视为国宝。地毯是土库曼斯坦最有代表性的手工艺品，各个民族都有自己独特的地毯纹饰。

　　土库曼斯坦流行的运动有足球、马术、摔跤等。

　　Rich in mineral resources, Turkmenistan is a country in the southwest part of Central Asia. The Monument of Neutrality expresses the Turkmen people's wish for peace and security. In Kunya-Urgench, a historical site demonstrates the nation's achievements in architectures and craftsmanship, and exhibits the once beautiful city. The Akhal-Teke, a Turkmen horse breed with a reputation for speed and endurance, is one of the oldest existing horse breeds worldwide. Turkmen carpets are a distinctive representation of Turkmenian handicrafts. Each ethnic group in Turkmenistan has its own distinctive design.

　　Sports favored by the Turkmen people include football, equestrianism and wrestling, etc.

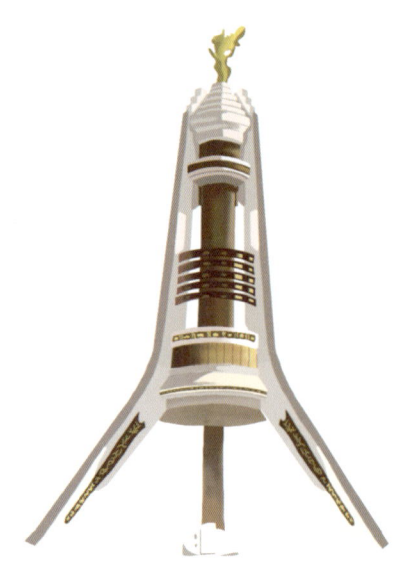

中立纪念碑

1995 年，联合国授予土库曼斯坦永久中立国地位；1998 年，土库曼斯坦建立了中立纪念碑。纪念碑的三个柱体撑脚分别代表独立、中立与民族团结。

Monument of Neutrality

The Monument of Neutrality was built in 1998 to commemorate the country's official position of neutrality given by the United Nations in 1995. The three legs of the arch symbolize independence, neutrality and national union respectively.

吉普恰克清真寺

位于首都阿什哈巴德市郊的吉普恰克村，总占地 36 万平方米，可容纳 10000 名朝圣者，规模宏大，被称为"土库曼斯坦伟大精神的象征"。

Gypjak Mosque

Located in the Gypjak village of the capital Ashgabat, the mosque covers a total area of 360,000 square meters and can accommodate 10,000 pilgrims. Being one of the largest mosques in Central Asia, it is considered as the "symbol of Turkmenistan spirit".

骆驼花轿

身着民族服装的土库曼斯坦男子牵着骆驼行走，骆驼的背上装有毛毯装饰的花轿，花轿里坐着美丽的少女，这是当地庆祝节日的活动之一。骆驼花轿也是土库曼斯坦迎娶新娘的传统仪式。

Camel Palanquin

The camel palanquin is one of the activities in local festival celebration and also a part of Turkmenistan's wedding customs. In this event, men dressed in traditional Turkmen attire lead camels adorned with decorative blankets, carrying a palanquin where a lovely maiden sits.

中 亚 Central Asia

苏丹帖乞失陵墓

库尼亚-乌尔根奇是中亚地区著名的古城之一，有着圆锥形绿松石圆顶的苏丹帖乞失陵墓是库尼亚-乌尔根奇的标志性建筑。

Sultan Tekesh Mausoleum, Kunya-Urgench
Kunya-Urgench is one of the famous ancient cities in Central Asia. The Sultan Tekesh Mausoleum with its conical turquoise dome is one of the landmarks in Kunya-Urgench.

阿哈尔捷金马

土库曼斯坦的国宝，世界现存最古老的马种之一，以速度和耐力著称。

Akhal-Teke
As the national treasure of Turkmenistan, Akhal-Teke is one of the most ancient horse breeds existing in the world, famous for its high speed and endurance.

地毯

土库曼斯坦素有"地毯王国"之称，其生活和文化都与地毯紧密相连。

Carpet
Turkmenistan is known as "Carpet Kingdom". The life and culture of Turkmenistan are closely linked with carpets.

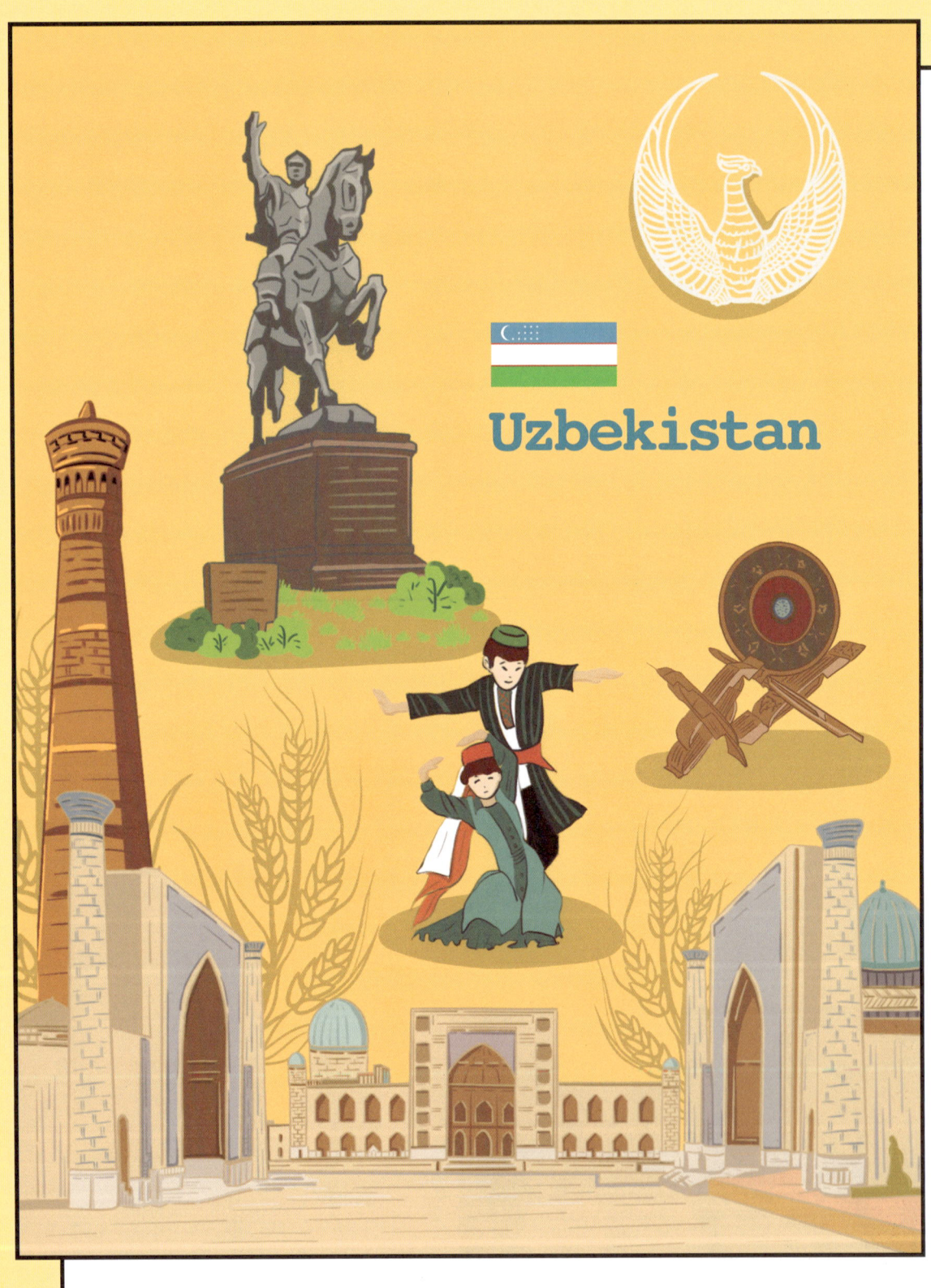

乌兹别克斯坦
Uzbekistan

全称乌兹别克斯坦共和国。乌兹别克斯坦位于中亚内陆地区，是世界上"双内陆国"之一。这里有引人入胜的古城和建筑，是丝绸之路上的璀璨明珠。这里的人们能歌善舞，热情友好。首都塔什干市中心矗立着民族英雄阿米尔·帖木儿骑马雕像。

乌兹别克斯坦流行柔道、摔跤等重竞技项目。

Full name: the Republic of Uzbekistan. Located in the interior region of Central Asia, Uzbekistan is one of the "double interior countries" in the world. With attractive architecture and ancient cities, it owns the reputation as the "pearl on the Silk Road". Good at singing and dancing, the Uzbeks are friendly and passionate. The statue of Amir Timur on horseback, the national hero of Uzbekistan, stands in the center of the capital Tashkent.

Judo, wrestling and other heavy athletics are popular in Uzbckistan.

列基斯坦神学院

位于撒马尔罕市中心，是一组由三座神学院组成的宏大建筑群，建于 15—17 世纪。

Registan

Lying in the heart of the ancient city Samarkand, the Registan consists of three madrasahs (Islamic schools). It was built between the 15th to 17th century.

喀龙宣礼塔

位于布哈拉市，建成时是中亚地区最高的建筑。宣礼塔用于召集信众祈祷。

Kalyan Minaret

Located in Bukhara, the Kalyan Minaret was the tallest architecture in Central Asia when it was built. The minaret was constructed to summon Muslims to pray.

中亚 Central Asia

阿米尔·帖木儿骑马雕像

位于塔什干市中心。阿米尔·帖木儿是乌兹别克斯坦著名历史人物，被视为民族英雄。

Statue of Amir Timur on Horseback
The statue is located in the center of Tashkent. Amir Timur is a famous historic figure who is considered a national hero in Uzbekistan.

木雕

乌兹别克斯坦人擅长的传统手工艺之一。

Wood Carving
Wood carving is one of Uzbek people's traditional arts.

传统舞蹈

乌兹别克斯坦的传统舞蹈伴随着有节奏感的音乐，舞者舞步轻盈、身腰柔软，不同地区的舞蹈具有不同的特点。

Traditional Dances
The traditional dances of Uzbekistan are accompanied by rhythmic music. The dancers have light steps and soft waists. The dances in different regions have different characteristics.

西 亚 West Asia

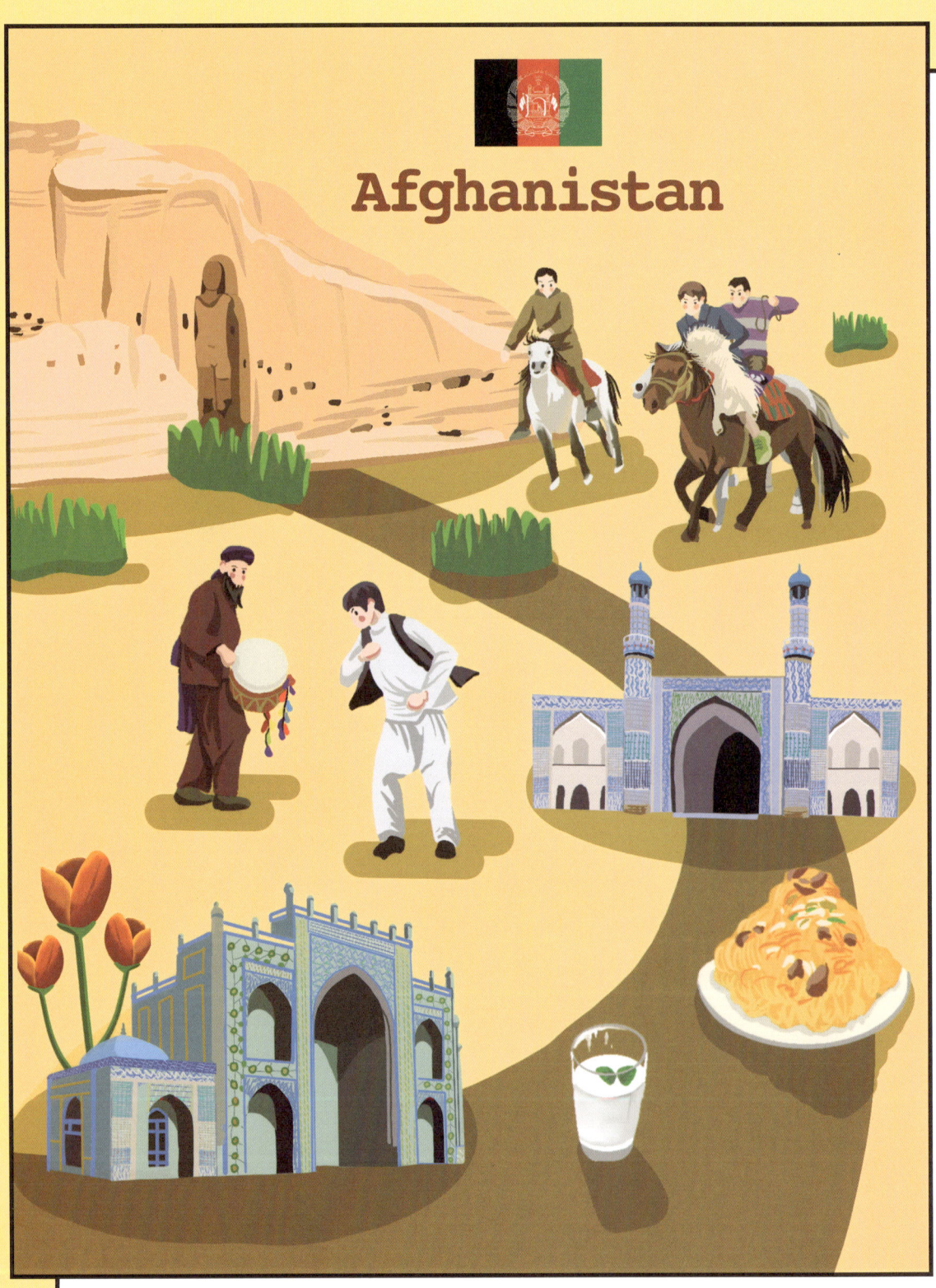

阿富汗
Afghanistan

全称阿富汗伊斯兰共和国。阿富汗是亚洲中西部的内陆国家。这里群山环绕，广袤的河谷地带花果飘香，阿富汗人骁勇的身姿在大地上奔腾。在赫拉特大清真寺和蓝色清真寺随处可见阿富汗人虔诚祈祷的身影，巴米扬山谷大佛和石窟展现了曾经的繁荣。阿坦舞是阿富汗的传统舞蹈。独具魅力的阿富汗文化虽历经风霜，但依然世代相传。

阿富汗流行的运动有足球、篮球、排球、手球、拳击等。

Full name: the Islamic Republic of Afghanistan. Afghanistan is an interior country in the central and western Asia. Surrounded by mountains, fragrance of flowers and fruits lingers in the vast river valleys. Bravely and valiantly, the Afghans gallop on the land. Piously praying Afghans can be seen in the Great Mosque of Herat and the Blue Mosque. The past prosperity is engraved in the Buddhas and grottoes of the Bamiyan Valley. Atan is the traditional dance of Afghanistan. Venturing through the vicissitudes of seasons, the charming Afghan culture has been inherited through generations.

Popular sports in Afghanistan include football, basketball, volleyball, handball, boxing, etc.

赫拉特大清真寺

又称贾米清真寺,位于阿富汗赫拉特省,是世界上著名的清真寺。

Great Mosque of Herat
Also known as the Jami Masjid of Herat, the Great Mosque of Herat is in the Herat Province of Afghanistan, and is a famous mosque worldwide.

蓝色清真寺

位于阿富汗北部的马扎里沙里夫市。清真寺由蓝色瓷砖镶嵌,因而被称作蓝色清真寺。

Blue Mosque
The Blue Mosque is located in the city of Mazar-I-Sharif in northern Afghanistan. Inlaid with blue tiles, the mosque is therefore known as the Blue Mosque.

巴米扬大佛

世界文化遗产,深藏在巴米扬石窟中。一尊身披红色袈裟,俗称"西大佛";一尊身披蓝色袈裟,俗称"东大佛"。

Buddhas of Bamiyan
Buddhas of Bamiyan is a World Cultural Heritage Site. The buddhas were carved in the grottoes along the Bamiyan Valley. The Western Buddha wore a red robe and the Eastern Buddha wore a blue robe.

马背叼羊

阿富汗北部盛行的一种骑在马背上的团队运动,被称为"国技"。两支队伍争抢一只被宰杀的羊,把抢到的羊扔到圆圈中,次数多的队伍获胜。

Buzkashi
Buzkashi, the national sport of Afghanistan, is a team sport prevailing in the northern region. Riding astride, two teams compete for the body of a slaughtered sheep and throw it into a circle. The team with the highest score wins.

西 亚 West Asia

阿坦舞

阿富汗传统舞蹈，是民族统一和独立的象征。一二百人围成圆形，舞蹈家在圆圈里随着节拍舞动。

Atan

Atan, the traditional dance of Afghanistan, signifies national unity and independence. One to two hundred people form a circle, and dancers dance along with the beat in the circle.

手鼓

杯状形状，常用于民族音乐中，是阿富汗的国家乐器。

Zerbaghali

Zerbaghali, a cup-shaped tambourine often played with folk music, is considered as the national musical instrument of Afghanistan.

郁金香

阿富汗国花，象征胜利和美好。

Tulip

Tulip, the national flower of Afghanistan, symbolizes victory and goodliness.

手抓饭

阿富汗人的主食，由米饭和盖浇的配料一起烹饪而成。

Kabuli Palaw

Kabuli Palaw is the main dish of Afghans, which essentially consists of steamed rice and various toppings.

酸奶饮料

一种用酸奶、薄荷、水做成的饮料，很受阿富汗人喜爱。

Doogh

Doogh, a beverage made of yogurt, mint and water, is very popular among the Afghans.

139

阿拉伯联合酋长国
The United Arab Emirates

阿拉伯联合酋长国位于阿拉伯半岛东部，北濒波斯湾，盛产石油。威严庄重的阿布扎比大清真寺闪耀着汉白玉的光彩，七星级帆船酒店矗立在波斯湾，奢华梦幻的棕榈岛展现迪拜的强大实力。阿拉伯羚羊在草原与沙漠间自由奔跑。落日为沙丘镀上灿烂的金色，冲沙运动刺激而奔放。

阿拉伯联合酋长国的传统运动有赛骆驼和驯鹰，民众喜爱足球、网球、板球等运动。

Situated on the east of the Arabian Peninsula, bordering the Persian Gulf to the north, the United Arab Emirates is rich in oil. The majestic Sheikh Zayed Mosque glows with white marble. The seven-star hotel Burj Al Arab rises on the Persian Gulf. The luxurious Palm Jumeirah demonstrates Dubai's reputation as a "leisure capital". Arabian oryx are running freely across grasslands and deserts. Golden sunset irradiates the sand dunes, where people take exciting desert off-road adventures.

Traditional sports of the United Arab Emirates are camel racing and falconry. Football, tennis and cricket, etc. are popular.

阿布扎比大清真寺

位于首都阿布扎比的两座桥梁——穆萨法大桥和马格达大桥之间,是阿拉伯联合酋长国最大的清真寺。

Sheikh Zayed Mosque
Sitting between two bridges—the Mussafah Bridge and the Maqta Bridge, in the capital city Abu Dhabi, the Sheikh Zayed Mosque is the biggest mosque in the United Arab Emirates.

帆船酒店

又名阿拉伯塔酒店,位于迪拜海湾。因外形酷似船帆,又称帆船酒店。

Burj Al Arab
Burj Al Arab is a luxury hotel located in the city of Dubai, also known as the Tower of the Arabs, with the shape resembling a sail.

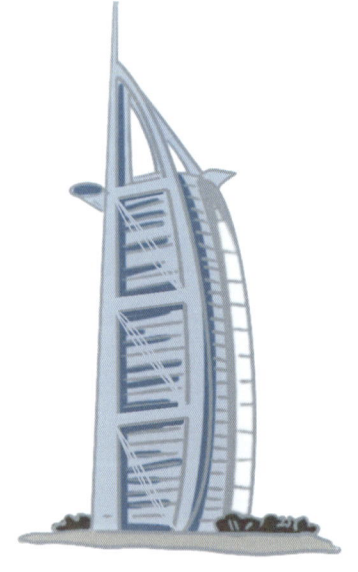

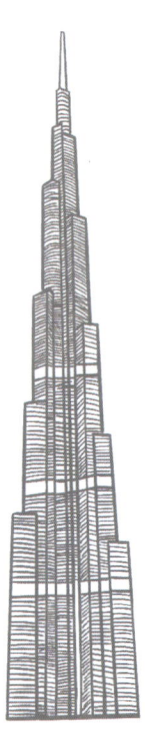

哈利法塔

原名迪拜塔,塔高 828 米,是目前世界第一高楼,也是迪拜著名景点。

Burj Khalifa
Formerly known as the Burj Dubai, the Burj Khalifa is 828 meters high and is currently the tallest tower in the world. It is also a famous attraction in Dubai.

西 亚 West Asia

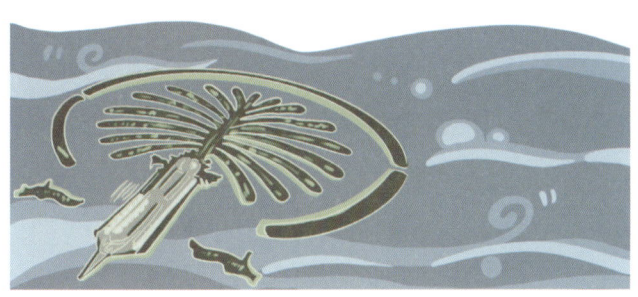

朱美拉棕榈岛

迪拜海岸的一个人工岛群，规模庞大，从空中俯瞰，形似棕榈树干。

Palm Jumeirah
Palm Jumeirah is a manmade archipelago on the coast of Dubai. It is huge and looks like a palm tree trunck from the air.

阿联酋航空

1985 年成立，以拥有国际化机组和现代化水平很高的机队而著称。

Emirates Airlines
Established in 1985, the Emirates Airlines is well-known for its international crew and the modern fleet.

沙漠冲沙

阿拉伯联合酋长国乃至整个阿拉伯地区非常受欢迎的民间运动。冲沙者可以驾驶越野车，也可以乘坐专门配置的吉普车，在沙峰沙谷间滑行。

Desert Off-road Adventure
Desert off-road adventure is a popular sport in the United Arab Emirates and even the Arab region. Adventurers can drive sport utility vehicles or take equipped jeeps to glide between peaks and valleys.

阿拉伯羚羊

国宝级野生动物，生活在干旱地区，特别是阿拉伯半岛一带，而今只在保护区内生活。

Arabian Oryx
Arabian oryx, a wile animal and national treasure, live in arid places especially the Arabian Peninsula. Now they only exist in sanctuary.

一分钟阅读

阿 曼
Oman

全称阿曼苏丹国。阿曼位于阿拉伯半岛东南部，濒临阿曼湾和阿拉伯海，据守印度洋通往波斯湾的门户。沙漠与海洋共同构成了阿曼别具一格的风景。在依山傍水的马斯喀特城，苏丹卡布斯大清真寺闪耀着伊斯兰文化的光辉，巴赫莱古代堡垒镇守着阿曼人世世代代的安宁。在这里，乳香沁人心脾，三角帆船迎风远航。

阿曼的传统运动有赛帆船、赛骆驼等。

Full name: the Sultanate of Oman. Bordering the Arabian Sea and the Gulf of Oman, Oman is a country on the southeastern Arabian Peninsula and serves as the gateway of the Indian Ocean to the Persian Gulf. Deserts and oceans together contribute to the distinguished scenery of Oman. In Muscat, a city encircled with mountains and sea, the Sultan Qaboos Grand Mosque shines with the brilliance of Islamic culture. Beside the oasis of Bahla, ancient forts safeguard the Omanis for generations. Frankincense refreshes people; dhows sail upwind.

Traditional sports in Oman include dhow racing, camel racing, etc.

苏丹卡布斯大清真寺

现代伊斯兰建筑，主要由大穹顶、主尖塔和四个侧翼尖塔构成。

Sultan Qaboos Grand Mosque

The Sultan Qaboos Grand Mosque, a modern Islamic architecture, consists of a central dome, the main minaret, and four flanking minarets.

巴赫莱城堡

阿曼现存著名的古城堡，世界文化遗产。

Bahla Fort

The Bahla Fort is the notable ancient fortress still existing in the country. It has been recognized as a World Cultural Heritage Site.

尼兹瓦城堡

阿曼固若金汤的城堡，也是阿曼现存古堡中保存最完整的古堡。

Nizwa Fort

The solid Nizwa Fort remains the most preserved one among extant historic forts in Oman.

西 亚 West Asia

马斯喀特城门博物馆

位于马斯喀特赛迪亚大街，2001年对外开放。博物馆建在城门之上，下方供车辆通行，上方供游客参观。博物馆展示了阿曼从新石器时代到现今的历史。

Muscat Gate Museum
The Muscat Gate Museum is located on the Al Saidiya Street in Muscat. Opened in 2001, the museum is constructed on a gate, with vehicles passing on the lower part and tourists visiting the upper part. The museum displays the history of Oman from the Neolithic Age to the present.

阿拉伯三角帆船

阿拉伯国家在濒临海湾的水面上有很多三角帆船，这些帆船被称为"阿拉伯三角帆船"。

Dhow
Along the coast of Arabian countries, there are quite many dhows—the traditional sailing vessels that are often with a triangular sail set.

乳香

采自橄榄科植物乳香树的芳香树脂，是阿曼文化不可分割的一部分。

Frankincense
Frankincense is a resin extracted from trees of the genus Boswellia in the family Burseraceae. It is considered to be closely connected with Omani culture.

阿曼咖啡

阿曼人经常饮用的饮料。阿曼人称咖啡为"喀赫瓦"。

Omani Coffee
The Omanis drink coffee frequently and call it "Kahwa".

一分钟阅读

巴勒斯坦
Palestine

　　全称巴勒斯坦国。巴勒斯坦位于亚洲西部，1988年建国。耶路撒冷是闻名遐迩的宗教"圣地"，世界三大宗教在此汇聚。耶稣印迹、犹太民族圣迹并存于巴勒斯坦的历史记忆中。圆顶清真寺是伊斯兰教的圣殿，寄托了巴勒斯坦人的信仰。大卫城塔下，古城依旧充满浓厚的宗教与历史底蕴。

　　巴勒斯坦流行的运动是足球。

　　Full name: the State of Palestine. Located in West Asia, Palestine was established in 1988. Jerusalem is a famous religious "shrine" where three religions assemble. Christianity and Judaism both exist in the historical memories of Palestine. The Dome of the Rock, an Islamic shrine, embodies the faith of Palestinians. Near the Tower of David, the Old City of Jerusalem still features a religious and historical atmosphere.

　　Football is popular in Palestine.

圆顶清真寺

坐落在耶路撒冷老城区，是伊斯兰教著名清真寺，耶路撒冷地标性建筑之一。

Dome of the Rock
Dome of the Rock is a famous Islamic mosque in the Old City of Jerusalem, and is one of the most renowned landmarks in Jerusalem.

哭墙

又称西墙，位于耶路撒冷旧城，是犹太教的圣迹。

Wailing Wall
In the old city of Jerusalem, the Wailing Wall, or the Western Wall, is a sacred monument of Judaism.

主诞堂

位于伯利恒。传说耶稣诞生于此地。

Church of the Nativity
The Church of the Nativity is located in Bethlehem. Traditionally it is believed to be the birthplace of Jesus.

西 亚 West Asia

大卫城塔

位于耶路撒冷，展示了过去纷乱的岁月。

Tower of David
Located in Jerusalem, the Tower of David represents the turbulent history of Jerusalem.

橄榄

巴勒斯坦盛产橄榄，橄榄是其重要的经济作物，同时也是和平与友谊的象征。

Olive
Palestine is rich in olives, which are an important cash crop. The olive is a symbol of peace and friendship.

瞪羚

濒危物种，拥有一双大眼睛，眼球向外凸起，看起来就像瞪着眼一样。

Gazelle
Gazelle is an endangered animal. It has particularly large eyes with eyeballs bulging outward, as if they are staring.

巴 林
Bahrain

全称巴林王国。巴林位于波斯湾西南部，由 30 余个岛屿组成，巴林岛为全国最大的岛。首都麦纳麦是海湾地区的金融中心，享有"波斯湾明珠"的美誉。麦纳麦大清真寺屹立于波斯湾海岸，巴林门守卫着麦纳麦入口，世贸中心大厦彰显巴林现代化魅力。生命之树在沙漠中不断生长。

巴林流行的运动有足球、田径、篮球、排球、赛车等。

Full name: the Kingdom of Bahrain. Bahrain is to the southwestern part of the Persian Gulf. Bahrain is the largest island among more than thirty islands which constitute the country. Enjoying the reputation of the "Pearl of the Persian Gulf", the capital city Manama is the financial center of the gulf region. The Al-Fatih Mosque Manama stands on the coast of the Persian Gulf; Bab Al Bahrain guards the entrance to Manama; the World Trade Center displays the modern charm of Bahrain. The Tree of Life thrives in the desert.

Popular sports in Bahrain are football, athletics, basketball, volleyball, auto racing, etc.

麦纳麦大清真寺

世界著名清真寺，能同时容纳 7000 多人。

Al-Fatih Mosque Manama

The Al-Fatih Mosque Manama pocesses the capacity to accommodate over 7,000 worshippers at a time. It is a world-famous mosque.

巴林门

位于麦纳麦前中央商务区海关广场的历史建筑，是麦纳麦集市的主要入口。

Bab Al Bahrain

Bab Al Bahrain is a historical building located in the Customs Square in the former central business district of Manama. It marks the main entrance to the Manama Souq.

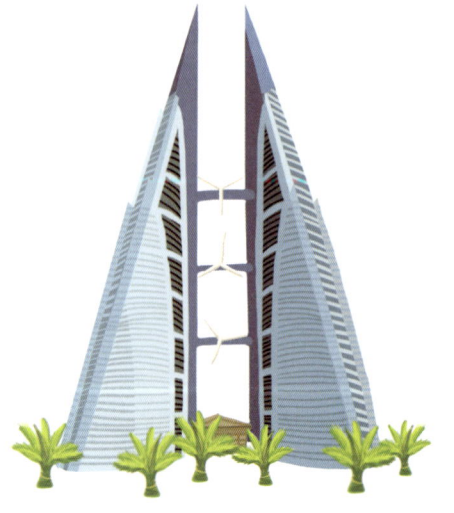

世贸中心

一座高 240 米、双子塔结构的建筑物，部分供电来自风力发电。

World Trade Center

The World Trade Center in Bahrain is a 240-meter-high twin tower complex with part of its energy supply coming from wind.

西 亚 West Asia

骆驼

被誉为"沙漠之舟",是人们载运重物穿越沙漠的交通工具。它能适应沙漠中的恶劣环境,具有极强的耐饥性和耐渴性。巴林有一个皇家骆驼农场,其中饲养了许多骆驼,免费开放给游人参观。

Camel
Known as the desert boat, the Camel is a means of transport for people to carry heavy loads across the desert. It can adapt to the harsh conditions of the desert and is highly resistant to hunger and thirst. There is a Royal Camel Farm in Bahrain with many camels and is open to visitors for free.

珍珠

在发现石油之前,巴林人以采捞珍珠和捕鱼为生。珍珠是巴林人的民族之魂和文化象征。

Pearl
Before oil was found, the Bahraini made a living by pearl diving and fishing. Pearls are the soul and cultural emblem of the Bahraini nation.

生命之树

巴林的沙漠地区中有一棵枝叶繁茂的树,四面沙丘没有其他植物生长,因此这棵树被当地民众誉为荒原上的"生命之树"。

Tree of Life
There is a lush tree in the desert area of Bahrain. Because it is the only major tree growing in the area, local people call it the "Tree of Life" in the wilderness.

卡塔尔
Qatar

全称卡塔尔国。卡塔尔位于亚洲西部,波斯湾西南岸的卡塔尔半岛上,南面与沙特阿拉伯接壤。首都多哈高楼林立,海滨灯火通明,洋溢着现代化的生机与活力。造型新颖的国家博物馆以"沙漠玫瑰"为原型,伊斯兰艺术博物馆静候远方来客。艺术精华在卡塔拉文化村汇聚,火炬酒店在海岸边熠熠生辉。

多哈曾经举办第15届亚运会(2006),2030年将举办第21届亚运会。卡塔尔人热爱的传统运动是冲沙、赛骆驼等。

Full name: the State of Qatar. Qatar is located in West Asia, occupying the Qatar Peninsula on the southwestern coast of the Persian Gulf, bordering Saudi Arabia to the south. Skyscrapers rise in the capital Doha. The corniche is illuminated brightly at night. Qatar is full of modern vigor and vitality. The National Museum of Qatar features its innovative appearance of the desert rose; the Museum of Islamic Art welcomes tourists worldwide. Art essence converges in Katara Cultural Village. The Torch Doha gleams on the coast.

The capital city Doha held the 15th Asian Games (2006) and will hold the 21st Asian Games in 2030. Traditional sports desert safari and camel racing, etc. are popular in Qatar.

国家博物馆

位于首都多哈，由老王宫改建而成，造型别致，浓缩了卡塔尔文化的精华。

National Museum of Qatar

Located in the capital Doha, the museum was established on the basis of the ancient palace. It has a unique appearance and encapsulates the essence of Qatari culture.

伊斯兰艺术博物馆

位于多哈，是以伊斯兰艺术为主题的博物馆。

Museum of Islamic Art

Located in Doha, the Museum of Islamic Art is a museum with the theme of Islamic art.

文化村鸽子塔

卡塔拉文化村是艺术胜地，最引人注目的是有很多洞的塔，鸽子喜欢聚集在这里。

Pigeon Towers of Katara Cultural Village

The Katara Cultural Village is a center of art. The most striking architecture is the Pigeon Towers with many holes, where pigeons like to assemble.

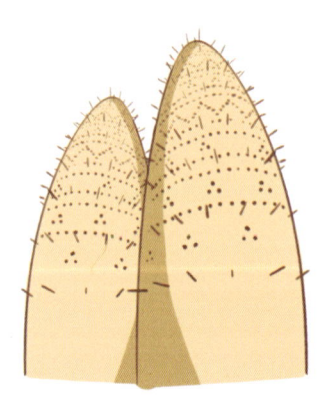

西 亚 West Asia

火炬酒店

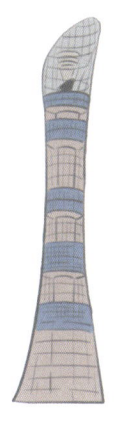

由 2006 年多哈亚运会火炬主塔改建成的一家五星级酒店，是多哈著名地标之一。

The Torch Doha
The Torch Doha, a five-star hotel renovated from the main torch tower of the Doha Asian Games in 2006, is one of Doha's famous landmarks.

阿尔达舞

卡塔尔民间舞蹈，过去表现战争题材，现在则在重要节日、婚礼庆典等场合表演。

Ardha
Ardha, a folk dance in Qatar, was historically a war dance. This dance is now usually performed on important festvials, wedding celebrations, etc.

独桅帆船

卡塔尔传统的木制独桅帆船，船体细长，在贸易史上曾经发挥过重要作用。

Dhow
Dhow, a traditional wooden sailing vehicle in Qatar, has mast and slender hull. Dhow played a significant role in Qatar's history of trade.

159

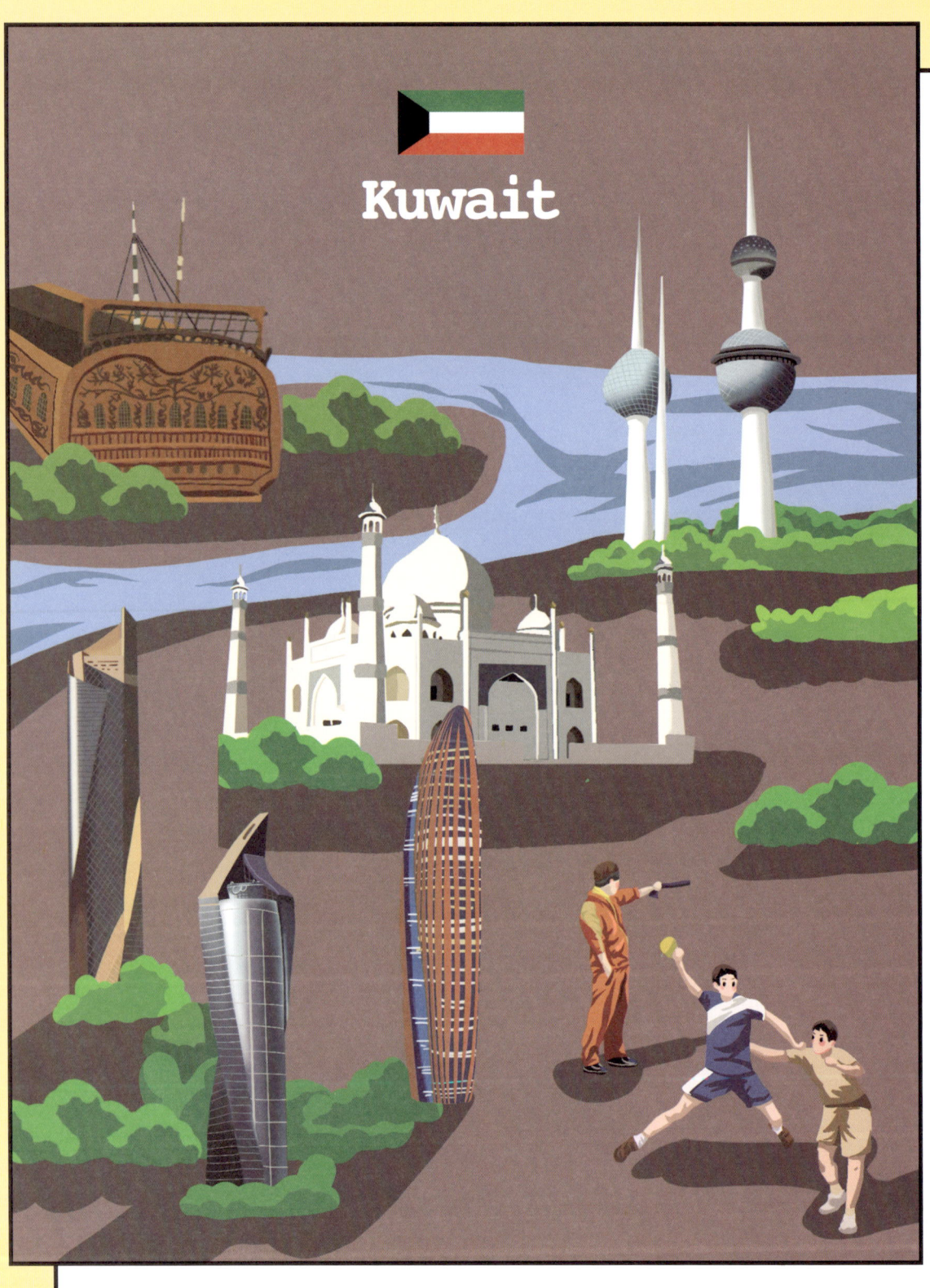

科威特
Kuwait

全称科威特国。科威特位于阿拉伯半岛东北部，波斯湾西北岸。丰富的石油和天然气资源助推了国家的现代化。法蒂玛清真寺装饰精致豪华，可容纳数千人礼拜；现代贮水塔集储水、旅游、观光功能于一体；豪华的木船饭店保留着阿拉伯的古代神韵。祖贝德鱼和椰枣仍是科威特人的重要食品。

科威特是西亚地区的体育强国，在射击、田径、手球等项目上颇具实力。

Full name: the State of Kuwait. Kuwait is a country on the northeastern Arabian Peninsula, northwest of the Persian Gulf. The wealth of petroleum and natural gas resources accelerates the modernization of this country. The gorgeous Siddiqa Fatima Zahra Mosque can accommodate thousands of people; Kuwait towers perform the functions of water supply and tourism; the luxurious Al-Hashemi-II maintains traditional Arabic charm. Zubaidi and date palm are still within Kuwaiti people's choices for food.

Kuwait is a leading sports country in West Asia, particularly in shooting, athletics, handball, etc.

法蒂玛清真寺

坐落于科威特国际机场附近的达希亚·阿卜杜拉·穆巴拉克市，于 2011 年建造完成。总面积约 3200 平方米，可容纳约 4000 人。

Siddiqa Fatima Zahra Mosque

Completed in 2011, the mosque is located in the city of Dahiya Abdullah Mubarak, near the Kuwait International Airport. The total area of the mosque is 3,200 square meters and it can accommodate approximately 4,000 people.

三座摩天大楼

"阿尔哈姆拉塔"是科威特第一高楼，总高度约 412 米，采用少见的卷曲造型，是一座办公大楼。另外，"科威特贸易中心"和"国民银行总部"两座摩天大楼也是科威特的地标性建筑。

Three Skyscrapers

The Al Hamra Tower is the tallest building in Kuwait. With a total height of 412 meters, it adopts a rare curl shape and serves as an office building. Besides, the Al Tijaria Tower and the NBK Tower are also iconic skyscrapers in Kuwait.

西亚 West Asia

科威特之塔

近代建筑史的杰作，位于首都科威特城，由3座高塔组成，集储水与观光于一体。

Kuwait Towers
The Kuwait Towers, a masterpiece of modern architecture, are located in Kuwait City. Three high towers integrate the functions of water storage and sightseeing.

萨斯饭店

科威特最豪华的木船饭店，是科威特标志性建筑之一。

Al-Hashemi-II
Al-Hashemi-II is the most luxurious wooden ship restaurant of Kuwait and the country's iconic landmark.

射击和手球

科威特的优势体育项目是射击，多次在国际赛事中取得好成绩。科威特手球队也是亚洲劲旅，亚洲手球联合会总部设在科威特。

Shooting and Handball
Kuwait's leading sport is shooting and Kuwait has achieved great results in shooting in many international competitions. The Kuwait national handball team is the powerhouse in Asia, with the headquarters of the Asian Handball Federation set in Kuwait.

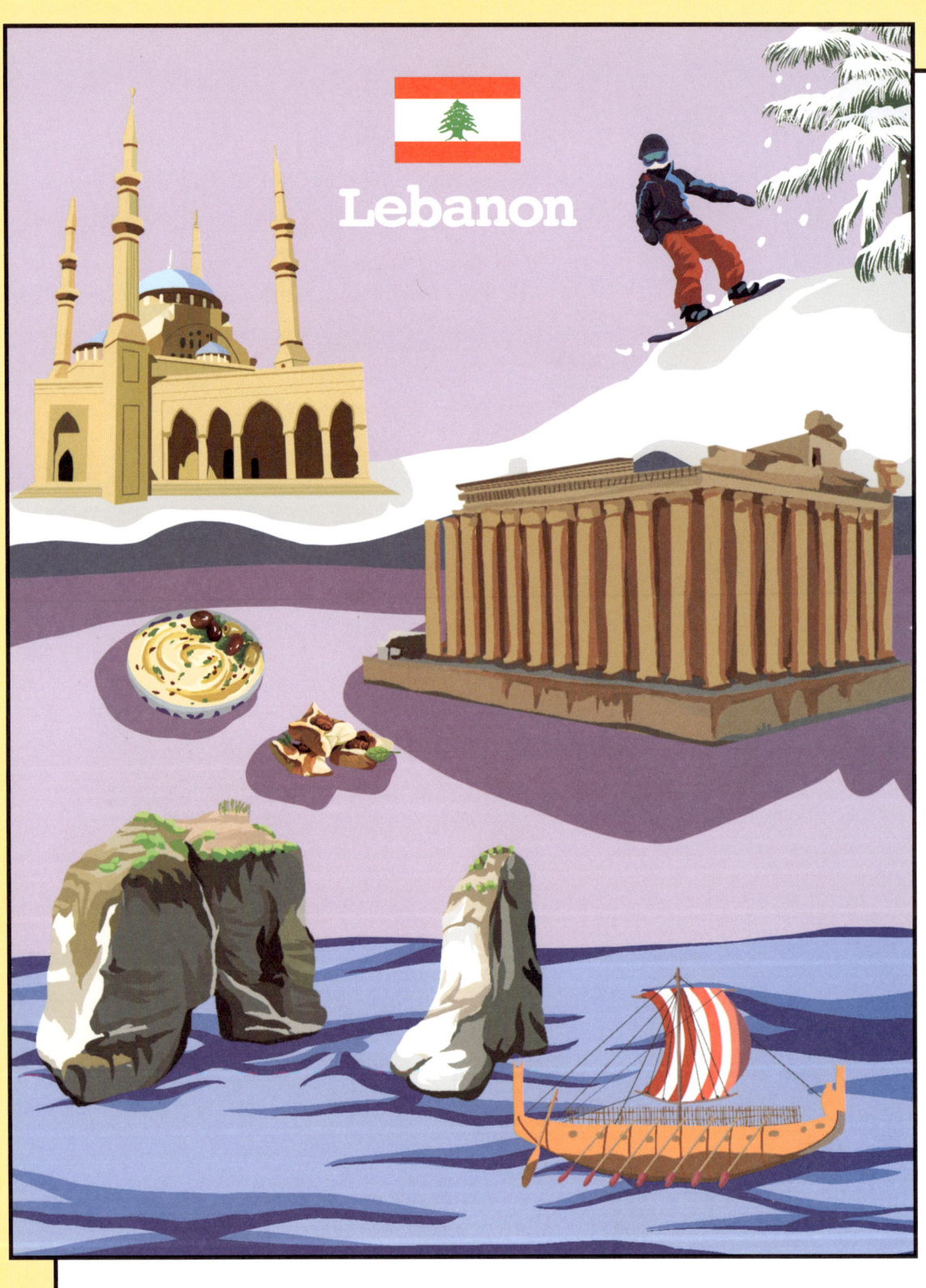

黎巴嫩
Lebanon

全称黎巴嫩共和国。黎巴嫩西濒地中海，东、北部接叙利亚，南邻巴勒斯坦、以色列。海洋与雪山遥遥相望，大自然赋予黎巴嫩旖旎风光。首都贝鲁特被誉为"东方的巴黎"。古代腓尼基人扬帆远航，曾经创造辉煌文明。巴勒贝克神庙历经风霜，是黎巴嫩悠久历史的见证者。清真寺和教堂并肩而立，多元文化是黎巴嫩独特的标志。

黎巴嫩流行的运动有足球、摔跤、滑雪等。

Full name: the Lebanese Republic. Bordering Syria to the east and north, Palestine and Israel to the south, Lebanon is a country on the eastern shore of the Mediterranean. The Ocean and snow mountains face each other across a distance. The nature endows Lebanon with a charming scenery. The capital city Beirut is known as the "Paris of the East". Sailing away, the Phoenicians created a splendid civilization. The Temple of Bacchus witnesses the rich history of Lebanon. Mosques stand side by side with churches, as multiculturalism is the distinctive feature of Lebanon.

The popular sports in Lebanon include football, wrestling, skiing, etc.

穆罕默德·阿明清真寺

黎巴嫩最大的清真寺，也是贝鲁特著名的地标建筑。巨大的圆顶和多个尖塔是其醒目的标志，圆顶上覆蓝色瓷砖。

Mohammad Al-Amin Mosque

The Mohammad Al-Amin Mosque is the largest mosque in Lebanon and the iconic landmark in the capital city Beirut. The huge dome and multiple spires are its marked signs. The dome is covered with light blue tiles.

巴勒贝克神庙

位于黎巴嫩首都贝鲁特东北部的贝卡谷地。崇拜太阳神的当地人修建了这座祭祀太阳神"巴勒"的庙宇。

Temple of Bacchus

The Temple of Bacchus is situated in the Bekaa Plain, northeast of the capital Beirut. The temple was built to dedicate to the sun-god "Baal" by local people who worshiped the god of the sun.

鸽子岩

贝鲁特的著名景点，岩体有波浪似的条纹，其中一块还有一个洞，像一座海上的石拱门，是观赏地中海落日的好地方。

Pigeon Rocks

The Pigeon Rocks is a famous tourist attraction in Beirut. The rocks have wave-like stripes and there is a hole on one rock which makes it resemble a stone arch on the sea. It is a wonderful place to enjoy the sunset in the Mediterranean.

雪松

黎巴嫩国树，象征着黎巴嫩人民坚忍的民族精神。

Cedar Tree

As the national tree of Lebanon, cedar tree symbolizes the resilient and unyielding national spirit of Lebanese people.

西 亚 West Asia

腓尼基船

古代腓尼基位于现今地中海东岸，黎巴嫩和叙利亚沿海一带。腓尼基人善于航海与经商，在兴盛时期曾经控制了西地中海的贸易，曾在北非等地区建立了许多殖民点。

Phoenician Ships

Phoenicia was an ancient region on the east coast of the present-day Mediterranean, corresponding to the coastal area of modern Lebanon and Syria. The Phoenicians were good at sailing and trading. In their heyday, they controlled the trade in west Mediterranean and established several colonies in North Africa.

馅饼

黎巴嫩传统美食，在地中海沿岸其他国家也很受欢迎，类似中国馅饼。馅料通常包括羊肉或牛肉，加上番茄、洋葱、松子等烹饪而成。

Sfiha

Similar to Chinese pie, Sfiha is a traditional dish in Lebanon and is also popular in the countries of the Mediterranean. Sfiha is cooked with minced meat, often lamb or beef, flavored with tomato, onion, pine nuts and so on.

鹰嘴豆泥

鹰嘴豆泥是一种涂抹式、蘸酱类的食品，由煮熟的鹰嘴豆或其他豆类与芝麻酱、橄榄油、柠檬汁、盐和大蒜混合制成。鹰嘴豆泥在黎巴嫩各类美食中占据了重要位置，可以搭配许多菜肴。

Hummus

Hummus is a dip, spread sauce. It is made from cooked chickpeas or other beans blended with tahini, olive oil, lemon juice, salt and garlic. Hummus plays an important role in Lebanese cuisine and can be served with a lot of dishes.

滑雪

滑雪运动在黎巴嫩盛行，黎巴嫩境内建有多个滑雪场。

Skiing

Skiing is popular in Lebanon. There are many ski resorts in Lebanon.

167

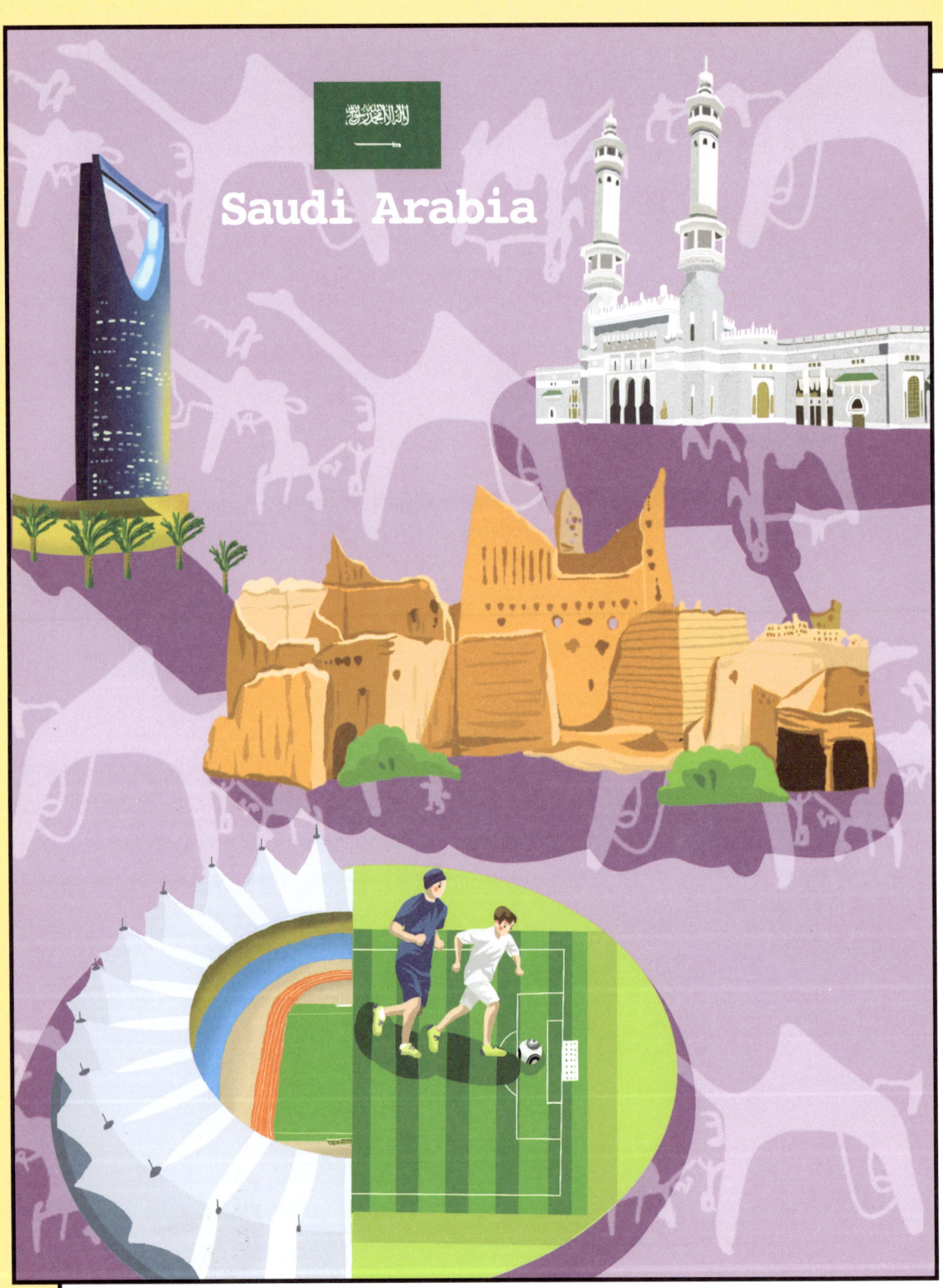

沙特阿拉伯
Saudi Arabia

全称沙特阿拉伯王国。沙特阿拉伯位于阿拉伯半岛，是世界石油输出大国。麦加大清真寺坐落于山峦环抱的麦加城，是全世界穆斯林朝觐的中心。阿图赖夫区是沙特家族的起源地，见证了沙特阿拉伯的历史文化。阿拉伯人的祖先在黑尔的岩石上留下了生动的历史印迹，岩画和碑文记录了先人们的活动。王国大厦矗立在首都利雅得的中心，法赫德国王国际体育场展现出沙特阿拉伯的现代风采。

沙特阿拉伯人喜爱足球运动，传统运动项目有赛马以及赛骆驼。

Full name: Kingdom of Saudi Arabia. Located on the Arabian Peninsula, Saudi Arabia is the world's largest oil exporter. As the largest mosque worldwide, the Great Mosque of Mecca sits in the center of Mecca, which is encircled by mountains. It is the site of pilgrimage for Muslims around the world. The At-Turaif District was the place of origin of the Saudi royal family, witnessing the history and culture of Saudi Arabia. Ancestors of Arabs left vivid historical marks on rocks in the Ha'il Region; petroglyphs and inscriptions recorded ancient activities. The Kingdom Center rises in the center of the capital city Riyadh. The King Fahd International Stadium presents the modern Arab charm.

Saudi Arabians like football. Their traditional sports are horse racing and camel racing.

麦加大清真寺

位于沙特阿拉伯麦加城中心，是伊斯兰教第一大圣寺。麦加是伊斯兰教的发祥地，是先知穆罕默德的故乡。

Great Mosque of Mecca

The Great Mosque of Mecca, located in the center of Mecca, Saudi Arabia, is a major site of pilgrimage in the Islamic world. Mecca is the birthplace of Islam and is supposed to be the birthplace of the Islamic Prophet Muhammad.

德拉伊耶遗址的阿图赖夫区

世界文化遗产，沙特王朝第一任首都所在地。

At-Turaif District in Ad-Dir'iyah

At-Turaif, the original home of the Saudi royal family, is a World Cultural Heritage Site.

黑尔地区岩石艺术

世界文化遗产。阿拉伯人的祖先在岩石上留下了岩画和碑文，记录了一万年前古人的生活。

Rock Art in the Ha'il Region

Rock art in the Ha'il Region is a World Cultural Heritage Site. The forebear of the Arabs left petroglyphs and inscriptions on the rocks' surface, recording the lives of people living 10,000 years ago.

西 亚 West Asia

王国大厦

沙特的标志性建筑,其设计能抵抗当地频发的沙尘暴,减少飓风对建筑物的影响。

Kingdom Center
The Kingdom Center, a landmark building in Saudi Arabia, has a special structure which helps to resist the ravage of frequent sandstorms and hurricanes.

法赫德国王国际体育场

位于沙特阿拉伯首都利雅得,是沙特阿拉伯国家足球队的主场。

King Fahd International Stadium
Located in the capital city Riyadh, the King Fahd International Stadium has been home to the Saudi Arabia national football team.

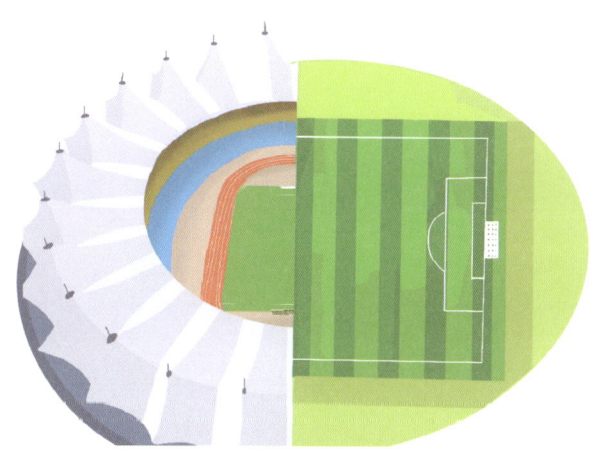

足球

沙特阿拉伯于1959年加入国际足联。国家男子足球队号称"西亚绿鹰"。

Football
Saudi Arabia joined FIFA in 1959. The Saudi Arabia national football team is known as "the Green Falcons".

叙利亚
Syria

全称阿拉伯叙利亚共和国。叙利亚位于亚洲西部，地中海东岸。古城逝去，遗址矗立，历史年轮在此刻下别具风格的印记。大马士革清真寺是伊斯兰建筑的瑰宝，阿勒颇城堡联结东西商贸往来，巴尔米拉古城凯旋门亲历古代都城繁华，水车在哈马城轮转。

叙利亚流行的运动有足球、篮球、游泳和网球等。

Full name: the Syrian Arab Republic. Syria is located in West Asia, on the east coast of the Mediterranean. History has faded away, while relics of the ancient city remains. Time has carved this land in a special way. The Umayyad Mosque is a treasure of Islamic architecture. The Citadel of Aleppo performed as the connection of east-west trade. The tetrapylon in Palmyra witnessed the prosperity of the old capital. Waterwheels spin in the city of Hama.

Popular sports in Syria are football, basketball, swimming and tennis, etc.

大马士革清真寺

坐落于叙利亚首都大马士革旧城中央,建于 705 年,是伊斯兰世界的经典建筑之一,也是世界清真寺的建筑范本。

Umayyad Mosque
The Umayyad Mosque is located in the center of the old city of the capital Damascus. Established in 705 AD, the mosque is a classic building in the Islamic world and is also the architectural model of mosques worldwide.

阿勒颇城堡

位于古老的中东城市叙利亚阿勒颇,是世界上历史悠久的城堡之一。

Citadel of Aleppo
Situated in Aleppo, which is one of the oldest cities in the Middle East, the citadel is regarded as a famous historical and cultural castle in the world.

巴尔米拉古城

巴尔米拉古城至今已有 2000 余年历史,是古代丝绸之路上的著名古城,也是一处世界文化遗产。凯旋门是巴尔米拉古城的标志性建筑。

Palmyra
Palmyra was a well-known ancient city on the "Silk Road", and has a history of more than 2,000 years. It is also a World Cultural Heritage Site. The tetrapylon is the iconic architecture in the Site of Palmyra.

西 亚 West Asia

哈马水车

叙利亚第四大城市哈马市以水车闻名,水车主要用于汲水灌溉农田,现已成为叙利亚哈马市的象征和特有的田间胜景。

Hama Waterwheel
Sitting on the banks of Hama, the fourth largest city in Syria, waterwheels are used to irrigate farmlands. Now, they have become the symbol of Hama and stand as the unique field scenery.

叙利亚棕熊

叙利亚棕熊是体形较小的一种棕熊,它的头大而圆,体毛粗密,肩背隆起,前肢力量很强。

Syrian Brown Bear
A Syrian brown bear is a small brown bear. It has a large and round head. Its fur is thick and dense. There is a bulging muscle on its back which gives the forelimbs strength.

茉莉花

叙利亚人对茉莉花怀有特殊的感情。大马士革几乎家家都栽茉莉花,芳香弥漫,是名副其实的"茉莉花之都"。

Jasmine
Syrians have a special affection for Jasmine. Nearly every household in Damascus keeps fragrant Jasmine which makes Damascus the "city of Jasmine".

乌德琴

西亚一带流行的传统拨弦乐器,琴身背部状似半个西瓜,弦轴箱自琴颈向后弯曲45到90度。

Oud
The Oud is a traditional plucked string instrument popular in West Asia. The back of the instrument resembles half of a watermelon, and the spindle box is bent backwards from 45 to 90 degrees from the neck.

一 分 钟 阅 读

也 门
Yemen

全称也门共和国。也门位于阿拉伯半岛西南端，西临红海，南濒阿拉伯海，是沙漠中的一颗明珠。巨石上的哈吉尔宫见证着也门的历史，首都萨那拥有"春城"的美誉。民居塔楼与清真寺穹顶比邻，高大的龙血树遥望满植于梯田的咖啡树。精美的腰刀和银质器具展现了也门高超的手工艺水平。

也门人热爱传统的体育运动跳骆驼，也喜爱现代足球和田径运动。

Full name: Republic of Yemen. Yemen is a country at the southwest end of the Arabian Peninsula, bordered by the Arabian Sea to the south and the Red Sea to the west, becoming a pearl of the desert. The Dar al-Hajar stands on a huge rock, witnessing the history of Yemen. The capital city Sana'a owns a reputation as the "Spring City". Multi-story dwelling buildings neighbor with mosques; tall Dracaena Cinnabari look over coffee trees widely planted in the terrace. The decorated jambiya and handmade silverware show the high level of the craftmanship of Yemen.

The Yemeni people like traditional camel jumping and modern sports, including football, athletics.

哈吉尔宫

也门著名的历史遗迹，位于距萨那 15 千米的达赫尔谷地，因建于一块巨大的岩石上，又被称为"石头宫"。曾经是也门王室宫殿，现为著名景点。

Dar al-Hajar

The Dar al-Hajar, a well-known historical site in Yemen, is located in the Wadi Dhar, 15 kilometers from Sana'a. It is also referred to as the "Stone Palace" as it stands atop a huge rock. Dar al-Hajar used to be a royal palace. Now it serves as a famous attraction.

萨那清真大寺

也门著名清真寺，位于首都萨那古城，建于 7 世纪，为一组圆顶式的阿拉伯古建筑群。在大寺的 12 扇大门中，有一扇还刻有希木叶尔文字。

Great Mosque

The Great Mosque, a famous ancient mosque in Yemen, lies in the old city of Sana'a and was built in the 7th century. It is a complex of domed Arab architectures. Among the twelve gates of the mosque, one is carved with Himyarite characters.

咖啡树和梯田

也门是世界上早期种植咖啡的国家之一，也门咖啡也被称为"摩卡咖啡"，以摩卡玛塔莉最负盛名。玛塔莉咖啡产自高海拔地区，也门人将咖啡树种植在梯田上，同时种植杨树给咖啡树提供生长所需的阴凉。

Coffee Tree and Terrace

Yemen is one of the earliest coffee-planting countries in the world. Yemen coffee is also called "Caffèmocha", with mocha matari being the most famous. Matari coffee is produced at high altitude. Yemeni grow poplar trees on terraces to provide shade for coffee trees.

西 亚 West Asia

龙血树

也门索科特拉岛最有名的独特植物,枝叶上翘形成一个倒伞形状的树冠。据说当龙血树受到损伤时,茎干会流出深红色的像血浆一样的黏液,因此得名。

Dracaena Cinnabari
The dracaena cinnabari is the most renowned and unique plant in Socotra Island. Its branches and leaves are upturned to form an inverted umbrella-shaped canopy. It is said that when the dracaena cinnabari is damaged, it will exude crimson blood-like mucus, hence the name.

宝瓶树

也门索科特拉岛中奇妙的风景线,它的树皮似皮革,巨大的块状根深入岩石,只需少量泥土即可生长。宝瓶树的花朵又被称为"沙漠玫瑰"。

Bottle Tree
Bottle trees are extraordinary scene in Socotra Island. The tree bark is like leather. The massive roots penetrate deeply into the rock and only a small amount of soil is enough for them to grow. The flowers of bottle trees are called the "desert roses".

腰带和腰刀

宽皮带和腰刀是也门男子的传统配饰,从前男子佩刀用于自卫,现在只为了装饰。在也门随便拔他人腰刀是一种禁忌。

Belt and Jambiya
In Yemen, men usually wear a wide belt and jambiya. The jambiya was worn for self-defense in ancient times, but now it is only for decoration. Drawing others' jambiya is considered a taboo in Yemen.

跳骆驼

"跳骆驼"就是人从几头骆驼身上跳过去,跳过骆驼数量多者获胜。这是也门独一无二的传统运动。

Camel Jumping
Camel jumping means jumping over several camels, and the one who jumps the most camels wins. It is a unique traditional sport in Yemen.

伊拉克
Iraq

全称伊拉克共和国。伊拉克位于亚洲西南部,阿拉伯半岛东北部。幼发拉底河和底格里斯河孕育了古代两河流域文明,这里也曾经是巴比伦王国的所在地。空中花园是闻名世界的建筑奇迹,古城遗址和螺旋宣礼塔是伊拉克悠久历史的见证,首都巴格达拥有厚重的历史文化底蕴。

伊拉克流行的运动是足球,其国家男子足球队曾被誉为"美索不达米亚雄狮"。

Full name: the Republic of Iraq. Iraq is located in southwestern Asia, the northeast of the Arabian Peninsula. The Euphrates River and Tigris River gave birth to the ancient Mesopotamian civilization. This is where the Kingdom of Babylon once stood. The Hanging Gardens is a world-famous architectural miracle. Ruins of ancient cities and the spiral minaret witness the long history of Iraq. Baghdad, the capital, has a rich historical and cultural heritages.

Iraqis like football. The Iraq national football team was known as the "Mesopotamian Lions".

哈特拉古城

哈特拉古城是古代帕提亚王国的一大军事重镇，也是重要的宗教和贸易中心。

Hatra
Hatra was an important military fortress of the Parthian Empire, and also a significant religious and trading center.

亚述古城

古代亚述帝国的都城，位于伊拉克北部，世界文化遗产。

Ashur
The ancient city of Ashur, the capital of the Assyrian Empire, is a World Cultral Heritage Site in northern Iraq.

螺旋宣礼塔

矗立在巴格达北部的萨马拉大清真寺广场，被列为全球十大螺旋楼梯之一。

Spiral Minaret
The Spiral Minaret rises on square of the Great Mosque of Samarra, north of Baghdad. It is listed as the top ten spiral stairway in the world.

西 亚 West Asia

特尔·阿斯玛尔宝藏

20世纪30年代,在埃什努那(现今阿斯玛尔)的一个神庙内发现了12尊雕像,被称为特尔·阿斯玛尔宝藏。这些雕像保存完好,大眼睛,据猜测可能是祭司或祈祷者。

Tell Asmar Hoard
The Tell Asmar Hoard is a collection of twelve statues unearthed beneath a temple in the 1930s at Eshnunna (now Tell Asmar). The statues, thought to be priests or worshippers, are well-preserved and have large eyes.

传统舞蹈

伊拉克传统民族舞蹈主要有甩发舞等。

Traditional Dance
Traditional folk dances in Iraq include Kwaleeya, etc.

空中花园

又称悬苑,古代世界七大奇迹之一,传说是巴比伦国王尼布甲尼撒二世为缓解王妃的思乡之情所建。空中花园采用立体造园的手法,园中种植各种花草树木,远看犹如花园悬在半空中。现已不复存在。

Hanging Gardens of Babylon
The Hanging Gardens of Babylon, also known as the Hanging Garden, one of the Seven Wonders of the Ancient World, is said to be built by Nebuchadnezzar II of Babylon for his consort, who was suffering from homesickness. It adopts a three-dimensional gardening method, and various flowers and trees are planted in the garden, which looks like a garden suspended in the air from a distance. It no longer exists.

一分钟阅读

伊 朗
Iran

全称伊朗伊斯兰共和国。伊朗位于亚洲西部，南濒波斯湾和阿曼湾。波斯帝国曾经留下辉煌历史，多种文明在时间的长河中绵延至今，书写下恢宏壮阔的华丽篇章。古列斯坦王宫的设计融合传统波斯工艺和欧式风格，精致奢华。莫克清真寺在彩釉装饰的渲染下，绚丽多彩。登上自由纪念塔，游客可以一览德黑兰城市风光。跳越篝火是伊朗的传统风俗，历久弥新。

德黑兰曾经举办第 7 届亚运会（1974），伊朗的体育强项是摔跤和举重。

Full name: the Islamic Republic of Iran. Iran is a country in Western Asia, bordering the Persian Gulf and the Oman Gulf to the south. It is a land where the Achaemenid Empire achieved its glory. A variety of civilizations met in the long river of time and Iran writes its own brilliant chapter. The extravagant Golestan Palace integrates traditional Persian craft with European style. Colorful stained glass irradiates the Nasir al-Mulk Mosque. From the top of the Azadi Tower, visitors could view the scenery of Tehran panoramically. Beside the bonfire, traditions of Iran persistently endure.

The capital city Tehran held the 7th Asian Games in 1974. Wrestling and weightlifting are Iran's famous sports.

古列斯坦王宫

世界文化遗产,一个庞大的王室官邸建筑群,德黑兰最古老的历史遗迹之一。

Golestan Palace
The Golestan Palace is a World Cultural Heritage Site and a vast complex of royal residences. It is one of the oldest historical relics in Tehran.

莫克清真寺

位于设拉子,建于 19 世纪,因其外墙彩釉以粉红色为主,也被称为"粉红清真寺"。

Nasir al-Mulk Mosque
Situated in Shiraz, the Nasir al-Mulk Mosque was constructed in 19th century. Thanks to the prominent pink color of the luster glazed on the outer wall, it is known as the "Pink Mosque".

自由纪念塔

位于德黑兰,1971 年 10 月落成。塔高 45 米,塔基长 63 米、宽 42 米,是德黑兰的地标和伊朗的象征。

Azadi Tower
Lying in Tehran with the height of 45 meters, the Azadi Tower was established in October 1971. The tower base is 63 meters long and 42 meters wide. It is a landmark of Tehran and the symbol of Iran.

西 亚 West Asia

跳火节

伊朗太阳历每年最后一个星期三是伊朗的传统节日"红色星期三",其中跳越燃烧的火堆是节日里的重头戏,因此也被称为"跳火节"。

Chaharshanbe Suri

The "Red Wednesday", a traditional festival of Iran, is the last Wednesday of a year in the solar calendar. As fire jumping is the highlight of the ceremony, the festival is also called Chaharshanbe Suri (the Fire Jumping Festival).

波斯猫

波斯猫起源于波斯,是最古老的猫种之一。

Persian Cat

Originated in Persia, the Persian cat is one of the oldest cat species.

鱼子酱

狭义上特指鲟鱼卵,是伊朗的主要出口产品之一。

Caviar

In a narrow sense, the caviar refers specifically to the sturgeon roe. It is one of the major export products of Iran.

塞塔尔

伊朗传统拨弦乐器,琴体呈小瓢形,琴杆细长。

Setar

The setar is a traditional musical instrument of Iran. A setar is a stringed instrument with a small scoop-shaped body and slender pole.

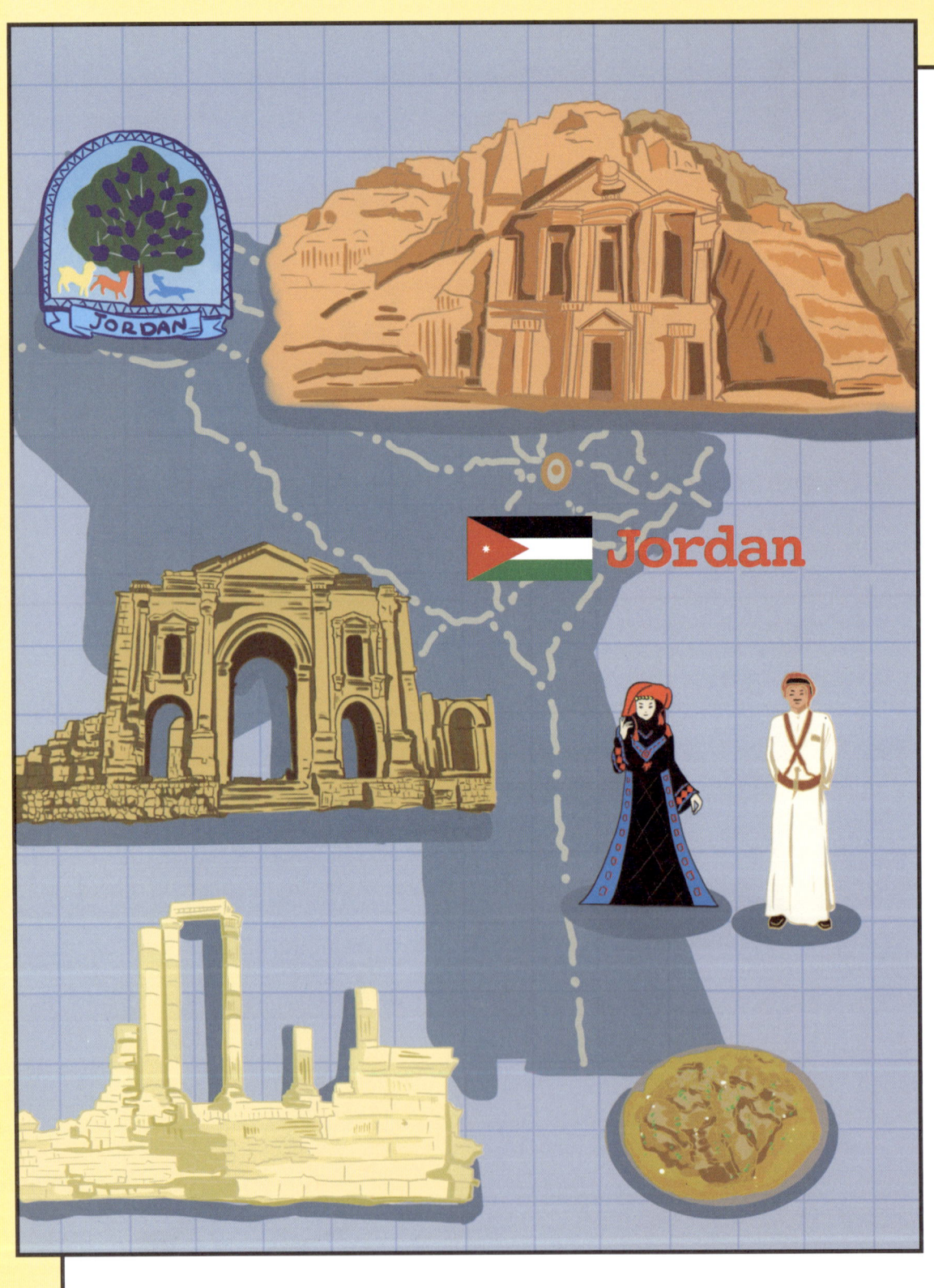

约 旦
Jordan

全称约旦哈希姆王国。约旦位于亚洲西部，阿拉伯半岛的西北部。深厚的历史积淀为约旦裹上古老而神秘的面纱。巍峨的群山下，古代文化遗址遍及全境。佩特拉古城历经千年而不失风采，杰拉什是约旦境内保存非常完好的古罗马城市，城堡山遗迹俯视安曼城。约旦汇聚古建筑艺术精华，留存着人类历史的珍贵回忆。

约旦流行的运动有足球、橄榄球、篮球、手球等。

Full name: the Hashemite Kingdom of Jordan. Jordan is located in West Asia, northwest of the Arabian Peninsula. Its rich history has veiled the land with antiquity and mystery. At the foot of stretching steep mountains, time-honored relics stand. For thousands of years, Petra maintains its precious beauty; Jerash is a very well-preserved ancient Roman city in Jordan; relics on the Castle Hill overlook the city of Amman. With essence of ancient architecture converging here, Jordan preserves precious memories of human history.

Popular sports in Jordan include football, rugby, basketball and handball, etc.

佩特拉古城

世界文化遗产，隐藏在一条连接死海和亚喀巴湾的峡谷中，曾经是古代西亚重要的商贸中心。

Petra

Petra, a World Cultural Heritage Site, situates in a gorge which links the Dead Sea and the Gulf of Aqaba. It was once an important trade center of West Asia in history.

杰拉什古城

位于约旦北部，是约旦境内保存非常完好的古罗马城市。古城中有一个为纪念罗马皇帝哈德良到访而建的哈德良门。

Jerash

Located in northern Jordan, Jerash is a very well-preserved ancient Roman city in Jordan. The Hadrian's Arch in Jerash was built in honor of the Roman emperor Hadrian's visit.

西 亚 West Asia

安曼城堡山

安曼的制高点，曾经是安曼最早的要塞。

Amman Citadel
The high ground of Amman, it was once the original fortress of Amman city.

曼萨夫

约旦传统菜肴，用发酵干酸奶酱烹制羊肉，搭配米饭或干小麦食用。

Mansaf
Mansaf, a traditional dish of Jordan, is made of lamb cooked with fermented dried yogurt sauce, served with rice or bulgur.

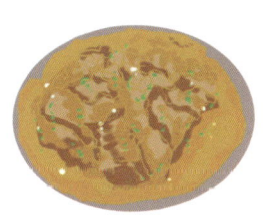

约旦传统服饰

约旦男人的传统服饰为一种长袖长袍，女人通常身着手工制作的刺绣长裙，戴头巾。

Traditional Jordanian Clothes
In Jordan, the traditional garment for men is dishdasha, which is a long-sleeved one piece robe. Women commonly wear handmade embroidered dresses with a hijab.

后 记

　　杭州亚运会不仅仅是一场体育盛会，也是一场亚洲国家和地区文化交流的盛会。本着促进亚洲各国文化交流、增强彼此理解与互信、构建人类命运共同体的信念，我们策划编著了此书，以期为杭州亚运会贡献一份力量。从项目启动到最终成稿，历时一年有余，文创工作室在资料查阅、内容筛选、文字撰写、语言翻译、绘图形式和版面设计等环节共同协作，不断商讨与修改，以期为公众呈现一本通俗易懂、知识丰富、质量上乘的亚洲文化读物。

　　在此，感谢杭州市相关部门和杭州师范大学科研部门的支持，也感谢全体文创团队成员的努力与付出，包括张卫良、林航、魏燕萍、韩千烨、张燕、颜晓霞和姚佳岚等同人的策划与构思，动画专业曾慧丹、彭越和谭翊的构图与绘制，鲁一帆和项紫微对部分图画的修正。最后，感谢浙江摄影出版社的编校制作。当然，本书仍存在种种不足，敬请读者批评指正。

Afterword

The Hangzhou Asian Games will not only be a sports event, but also a grand event for cultural exchanges between Asian countries and regions. To promote the mutual understanding and a sense of community in Asian countries and regions, we initiated this project for the Hangzhou Asian Games. Our Cultural and Creative Studio worked together in material selection, literal expression, translation, drawing form and layout design, so as to present to the public an easy-to-understand, accurate and high-quality book on the cultures of Asian countries and regions.

We hereby give thanks to relevant Hangzhou municipal departments and the Scientific Research Department of Hangzhou Normal University. We also thank all members in the Cultural and Creative Studio for their contribution. The planning of this project was undertaken by Zhang Weiliang, Lin Hang, Wei Yanping, Han Qianye, Zhang Yan, Yan Xiaoxia and Yao Jialan. Zeng Huidan, Peng Yue and Tan Yi of the Animation Department contributed to the designing and completion of all pictures. The final correction and alteration of selected pictures was completed by Lu Yifan and Xiang Ziwei. Last but not least, for the dedication and contribution of Zhejiang Photographic Press, we give our sincere appreciations. For the Inevitable shortcomings in the book, any comment or corrections are highly appreciated.

致 谢

本书获得如下资助:

杭州市哲学社会科学重点研究基地、杭州城市国际化研究院(中心)重点课题资助：项目编号 2022JD26。

杭州师范大学人文社科振兴计划新型智库建设"城市发展与战略研究"项目资助。

Acknowledgement

This book is funded by:

Key Program of the Hangzhou Philosophy and Social Science Key Research Base, IHI: 2022JD26.

New Think-Tank Construction Program "Urban Development and Strategy Research", The Humanities and Social Science Revitalization Project, Hangzhou Normal University.

责任编辑：姚成丽　王梁裕子
装帧设计：秦逸云
责任校对：高余朵
责任印制：汪立峰

图书在版编目（CIP）数据

亚运文化之旅：杭州亚运会参赛国家和地区文化知识双语绘本：汉语、英语 / 杭州城市国际化研究院文创工作室编绘. -- 杭州：浙江摄影出版社，2023.7
 ISBN 978-7-5514-4575-7

Ⅰ. ①亚⋯ Ⅱ. ①杭⋯ Ⅲ. ①文化史－亚洲－通俗读物－汉、英 Ⅳ. ①K103-49

中国国家版本馆CIP数据核字(2023)第114553号

YAYUN WENHUA ZHI LÜ: HANGZHOU YAYUNHUI CANSAI GUOJIA HE DIQU WENHUA ZHISHI SHUANGYU HUIBEN

亚运文化之旅：杭州亚运会参赛国家和地区文化知识双语绘本

杭州城市国际化研究院文创工作室　编绘

全国百佳图书出版单位
浙江摄影出版社出版发行
　　地址：杭州市体育场路 347 号
　　邮编：310006
　　电话：0571-85151082
　　网址：www.photo.zjcb.com
制版：浙江新华图文制作有限公司
印刷：浙江兴发印务有限公司
开本：787 mm × 1092 mm　1/16
印张：12.75
2023 年 7 月第 1 版　2023 年 7 月第 1 次印刷
ISBN 978-7-5514-4575-7
定价：88.00 元